G000124806

EDUCATION IN A COMPETITIVE AND GLOBALIZING WORLD

REFORMING EDUCATION IN CONTEMPORARY MACAO

ISSUES AND CHALLENGES

EDUCATION IN A COMPETITIVE AND GLOBALIZING WORLD

Additional books in this series can be found on Nova's website under the Series tab.

Additional e-books in this series can be found on Nova's website under the e-book tab.

EDUCATION IN A COMPETITIVE AND GLOBALIZING WORLD

REFORMING EDUCATION IN CONTEMPORARY MACAO

ISSUES AND CHALLENGES

YI-LEE WONG
AND
CHI-FONG CHAN

New York

Library of Congress Cataloging-in-Publication Data

ISBN: 978-1-63321-912-0

Published by Nova Science Publishers, Inc. † New York

CONTENTS

About the Authors

Yi-Lee Wong
Assistant Professor,
Faculty of Education
Chinese University of Hong Kong
Hong Kong, P. R. China

Chi-Fong Chan
Associate Professor
Centre of Continuing Education and Special Projects
Macao Polytechnic Institute
Macao, China

ACKNOWLEDGMENTS

This book is our collaboration in bringing together different research projects that we have been doing on education in contemporary Macao to address some hotly debated educational issues in Macao. In completing this book, we are deeply indebted to many people for their assistance and support. We would like to thank our affiliated institutions where we are working, and worked, while finishing up this book for giving us an abundance of support: Yi-Lee Wong would like to thank the Faculty of Education, University of Macau (2009-2013) and the Faculty of Education, Chinese University of Hong Kong (2013-now) and Chi-Fong Chan would like to thank the Centre of Continuing Education and Special Projects, Macao Polytechnic Institute.

Apart from getting such important institutional support, we have been fortunate that many individuals are being extremely helpful in introducing us to respondents qualified for our projects, and also that the respondents of different projects are so generous about their time sharing with us their valuable knowledge and precious experiences. But for the assistance of those many individuals and the generosity and kindness of the respondents, our projects would have been impossible; needless to mention, there would have been no way to complete this book. A BIG thank-you goes to all of those helpful individuals. And, we are deeply grateful to our respondents.

Last, but definitely not the least, we would like to thank our families for their inspiration and support of various forms.

Yi-Lee Wong and Chi-Fong Chan

August 2014
Hong Kong and Macao

Chapter 1

INTRODUCTION

Over the past several years, Macao has made the headlines of many international newspapers due to its astronomical Gross Domestic Product (GDP) figures. Almost as widely noted has been Macao's high student retention rate in schools.

According to the Programme for International Student Assessment (PISA) in 2009, over 40% of 15-year-olds have been retained. But within Macao a number of educational issues aside from grade retention have attracted public debate: the low completion rate of basic education, the quality of the education itself, the pay and benefits of teachers in private schools, and the professionalism of teachers in general.

Macao is often presented as a society where people live in harmony, and teachers as the "calmest professionals", but even teachers joined the mass demonstration on the first of May in 2011 to fight for better pay and their professional dignity.

In March 2012, 'The legal frame for regulating teachers hired by private schools' (hereafter referred to as the Private Legal Frame) was finally passed after almost two decades of debate. Since then, certain unintended consequences of the Private Legal Frame have become issues for public discussion.

What is unclear is why these issues in education have become such pressing concerns in Macao. More specifically, why has education become such an issue and what is at stake? How should we make sense of these issues? What can be done to address them?

Finally, where the development of education is concerned, what can we learn from the case of Macao?

MAJOR CONCERNS

In order to make sense of these issues, we have to put them in context: the immediate context of Macao's education system and the wider social, political, and historical context of Macao. An understanding of the operation of the Macao education system and the history and the social and political development of Macao are prerequisites for having a sensible discussion about education in Macao. By examining educational issues such as high grade retention and the low completion rate of basic education in Macao, this book aims to identify challenges facing the system of basic education in Macao in particular and the challenges facing Macao in general. After the 1999 handover to the People's Republic of China (PRC) and the setting up of the Macao Special Administrative Region (SAR) government, the provision and the quality of basic education in Macao has been improved. However, these improvements have not solved the perennial problems of education in Macao. The high grade-retention and low completion rate of basic education are both legacies of the colonial neglect of education for the local Chinese by the Portuguese colonial government in Macao. Given such colonial neglect and the impact of this legacy on the subsequent development of education in Macao, the quality of basic education has been a pressing issue. As will be shown in the subsequent chapters, the efforts of the SAR government to standardize and/or regulate the practices of schools have not prevented the Macao education system from remaining effectively a network of private schools.

The autonomy of private schools and the freedom of such schools to operate in their own style are guaranteed by the Basic law, and are a holdover from Portuguese colonial rule. Even after the 1999 handover, private schools retained their distinctive management styles and have resisted any attempt by the Macao SAR government to centralize and regulate their curriculum, pedagogical practices and assessments, or their management of teachers and students. Such schools object in the name of freedom to adopting a standardized examination system, and indeed it remains debatable whether to implement a standardized examination for all students in Macao. These schools also tend to operate a didactic approach in the classroom, for ease of student management. Although the Macao SAR government has sought to provide more resources and support to improve the quality of teacher training and enable the professional development of teachers, schools can still hire teachers to their liking without necessarily considering whether they are qualified, let alone professional. Equally, schools are under no obligation to improve the contracts of teachers, so can hire teachers on an undignified package, renew contracts with teachers annually rather than giving tenure, and fire them without legal obligation to provide sensible reasons. In short, the financial situation and the job security of teachers have not been greatly improved, with teachers remaining at the disposal of school principals. Simultaneously, the professionalism of teachers in Macao is still in serious doubt. And again, in the name of defending their autonomy, private schools are not obliged to review their school regulations (including the criteria for grade retention and disqualification) however outdated or unreasonable the regulations may seem. All these circumstances play different roles in making sense of a high rate of grade retention and a low completion rate of basic education in Macao.

Data and Sources of Information

In order to systematically discuss the educational issues raised here, we have sought to pool various sources of information. Some provide a general background of education in Macao and other offer specific insights towards a better understanding of the operation of the Macao education system. In general, four types of information will be used as data in this book: data from secondary sources; findings from five research projects; newspaper clippings from a major local newspaper in Macao; and observations and personal communication of the first author from time spent teaching at the Faculty of Education, University of Macau. While information of these four types serves different purposes, we seek to make use of them to engage in a constructive discussion of education in Macao.

Secondary Data

Data from secondary sources refer to the documents and statistics about education in Macao from various local organizations (non-official), including data from existing international studies such as PISA, and official documents and statistics available on the websites of the Government of Macao Special Administrative Region Statistics and Census Service (http://www.dsec.gov.mo) and the Education and Youth Affairs Bureau (http://www.dsej.gov.mo). The documents and statistics about the historical development of education in Macao have mainly been collected by the second author, who is an expert in the history of education in Macao. In fact, a number of official statistics about education in Macao over the last decade were in fact compiled by the second author (Chan, 2010). Such secondary data serve to provide us with a general background for making sense of the educational issues discussed in this book.

Five Research Projects

In addition to this general background, derived from the abovementioned secondary sources, we shall make use of some specific findings derived from five research projects.

One was conducted by the second author: a two-year study of the oral history of eight retired school teachers in Macao. Through examining the life histories of the school teachers, the second author seeks to provide insights into understanding the development of basic education in Macao since the Second World War. The other four projects were conducted by the first author with the help of the second author and several student researchers from the University of Macau.

Table 1.1. Research projects conducted by the first author

Research project	Specific concern	Month of commencement
Educational inequality in Macao: How do high-school students make educational choices?	To examine class effects and school effects in students' educational choices in Macao	January 2010
Stories of evening-school students in Macao: Why quit? Why return?	To explore the applicability of the concepts of 'cultural capital' and 'resistance' in making sense of the schooling experiences of evening-school students in Macao	September 2011
School management in Macao: Regulation of students and teachers	To examine the mechanisms through which students and teachers are regulated at school in Macao	March 2012
School dropouts in Macao	To examine how students become school dropouts in Macao	March 2013

The first author began her research into education in Macao on joining the University of Macau in 2009. The four projects, different yet related, were not conducted one after another but followed a rough chronological sequence. The first project is about how and why high-school students in Macao make particular educational choices. The second project samples the stories of evening-school students on their decisions to quit mainstream schooling and their eventual return to education. The third project is about the regulation of students and teachers by schools. This project includes a textual analysis of school regulations and teacher manuals, soliciting views from students on school regulations, and views from teachers on school regulations and teacher manuals. Finally, the fourth project is about the schooling experiences of school dropouts. Table 1.1 lists the four research projects and provides a brief description of each.

While data collection for the first three projects conducted by the first author is completed, the first author continues to work on recruiting school dropouts and arranging interviews with them. While there are four projects, three major study targets can be distinguished: texts, teachers, and students. Table 1.2 summarizes and arranges these projects by those study targets. The first type of study targets are texts: school regulations and teacher manuals. In order to understand the relationships between teacher and student, between students and their school, between schools and their teaching staff in particular, and the management of schools in general, it is necessary to examine the school regulations and teacher manuals that set these relationships out in black and white. In particular, the criteria for grade retention set by schools could enable us to make sense of how grade retention operates in Macao. More generally, this analysis sheds light into what kind of control schools seek to exert over teachers and students, thereby giving us better ideas of the atmosphere of schooling in Macao. In addition, this analysis enables us to examine what qualities schools seek to cultivate in students and what kind of teachers schools expect their teaching staff to be.

The study targets of the second type are teachers. We seek to solicit views from teachers on the regulation of students and teachers by schools. We focus especially on teachers' views and practices in relation to school regulations in general and grade retention in particular.

To this end, we conducted a survey and then a series of focus-group interviews. For the survey, teachers from two different sources were recruited to fill in a questionnaire with mostly closed questions: these were teachers

Table 1.2. Study targets of the four research projects conducted by the first author

Study targets	Research project	Period of data collection
Texts		
1. School regulations	To examine school regulations in Macao to see what kind of students the schools seek to nurture or what qualities the schools seek to cultivate in students	School regulations of all primary and secondary schools collected between January and March 2013
2. Teacher manuals	To examine teacher manuals to see what sort of control the schools seek to exert on teachers and to examine the relationship between teachers and schools	Teacher manuals of some secondary schools collected between March and June 2013
Teachers	To conduct survey research with teachers to see how they view school regulations	Questionnaires were distributed to three schools in May 2012 and two classes of Post-Graduate Diploma in Education in June 2012. Completed questionnaires collected in May 2013
	To conduct focus-group interviews with teachers to see their views on school regulations (specifically grade retention) and on teacher manuals and teachers' relationship with schools	Focus-group interviews were conducted between March and June 2013
Students		
1. Senior-secondary-form-three students	To conduct semi-structured interviews with them to examine their considerations underlying their educational choices	Face-to-face interviews were conducted between July 2010 and March 2011
2. Evening-school students	To conduct semi-structured interviews with them to examine their stories of quitting schooling and returning to education	Face-to-face interviews were conducted in December 2011
3. School dropouts	To conduct semi-structured interviews with them to examine their educational experiences (how they become dropouts)	So far eight face-to-face interviews were conducted in June 2013 (recruitment and interviews are still going on)
4. Secondary school students aged 15 or above	To conduct focus-group interviews with students to see their views on school regulations (especially grade retention).	Focus-group interviews were conducted between March and June 2013

from three selected schools (one top-ranking, one middle-ranking, and one low-ranking) and teachers of two classes reading a Post-Graduate Diploma in Education (PGDE) programme for in-service teachers run by the University of Macau. Questionnaires were distributed to the three schools in May 2012 and to the two classes during the last lectures in June 2012.

All questionnaires were collected in May 2013. In total 202 completed questionnaires were collected. The distribution of teachers is summarized in Table 1.3.

Table 1.3. The sample of teachers completing the questionnaire on school regulations

Source of teachers recruited	Number of teachers
A selected top-ranking secondary school	40
A selected middle-ranking secondary school	71
A selected low-ranking secondary school	47
Two classes of Post-Graduate Diploma in Education programme run by the University of Macau for in-service teachers	44
Total	202

In addition to the survey, we also conducted a series of focus-group interviews with teachers. Four types of schools were identified (see Appendix A for the full list of secondary schools by type), because, as will be discussed, schools of each type design similar school regulations. Using quota sampling, we sought to recruit 5 teachers from each type of school for focus-group interviews. However, given the small number of government schools (indicated in Table 1.4 below), it was very difficult to recruit teachers teaching in government schools. In the end, 24 teachers were recruited but none from government schools. Table 1.4 reports that 9 teachers are from schools run by traditional organizations, 8 from schools organized by the Catholic Church, and 7 from other schools. Two taped focus-group interviews were arranged for teachers from schools of each type. In the first interview, teachers were asked to share and discuss their views on grade retention and their practices related to grade retention at school. In the second interview, teachers were asked to share and discuss their views on the management of teachers by schools and the relationships between schools and their teaching staff (see Appendix B for the interview schedule for the two sessions of interview). In total, six focus-group interviews with teachers from the three types of schools were conducted between March and June 2013.

Table 1.4. Four types of schools in Macao and composition of the teacher sample for the focus-group interviews

School type	Number of primary schools	Number of secondary schools	Number of teachers recruited
Schools organized by traditional organizations	23	15	9
Schools organized by the Catholic Church	23	16	8
Government schools	5	3	0
Other schools	13	9	7
Total	64	43	24

The study targets of the third type are students. As mentioned above, there are actually three projects about students. The first targets high-school students: officially speaking, they are senior-secondary-form-three students (students doing the last year of secondary education). The major focus of this project is on how they make educational choices, but their educational experiences are also of relevance. In recruitment, three secondary schools (out of 43) were selected according to their ranking – from top-ranking, middle-ranking, and low-ranking schools respectively. After the schools were selected, quota sampling was used to recruit 15 senior-secondary-form-three students from each school. Finally, 48 senior-secondary-form-three students were recruited: 19 students from the top-ranking school, 13 from the middle-ranking one, and 16 from the low-ranking one. Interviews were conducted between July 2010 and March 2011. In each interview, the 48 students were asked to talk about their schooling experiences and relationships with classmates and teachers, their relationships with parents and parental support received, their educational aspirations and educational plans, and their views on the Macao education system and social competition in Macao (see Appendix C for the interview schedule).

The second project targets evening-school students: officially speaking, they are in junior secondary form three (students doing the last year of junior secondary education) or in senior secondary form three. In Macao, nearly all secondary schools are day schools. While day schools are designed for students of the relevant age group, evening schools are designed to provide a basic education for students of any age who have missed an opportunity for education but would like to return to education (this is called 'recurrent education' in Macao). In this project, the first author sought to look into the 'stories' of evening-school students to trace their educational trajectories. After an evening school was selected from potential nine schools, 18 evening-school students were recruited: 12 from senior secondary form three and 6 from junior secondary form three. Interviews were conducted in December 2011. In each interview, the 18 evening-school students were free to tell their stories of how they quit schooling and then decided to return to education (see Appendix D for the interview schedule).

Table 1.5. A brief description of students included in this book

Types of students	Number
Senior-secondary-form-three students from a selected top-ranking secondary school	19
Senior-secondary-form-three students from a selected middle-ranking secondary school	13
Senior-secondary-form-three students from a selected low-ranking secondary school	16
Secondary school students from a selected evening school	18 (12 in senior secondary form three and 6 in junior secondary form three)
School dropouts	8
Secondary school students aged 15 or above for focus-group interviews	29
Total	103

The third project targets school dropouts. Technically speaking, these are students aged below 18 who quit schooling before completing a fifteen-year compulsory education. This project was started in June 2013 and is still going on. It seeks to examine the educational experiences of school dropouts (see Appendix E for the interview schedule) in order to further our understanding of the operation of schools in Macao. Two organizations were contacted, from which 10 subjects have so far been recruited. Eight school dropouts were interviewed in June 2013. In order to compare their views on school regulations, especially grade retention, with students still in the education system, focus-group interviews were arranged for students aged 15 or above. 29 students were recruited for this purpose and interviewed between March and June 2013. Table 1.5 provides a brief description about students included in the discussion in this book.

In addition to carrying out these research projects, the first author also arranged informal interviews with some teachers from the three selected secondary schools and the selected evening school. She also conducted a joint interview with two teachers who participated in teacher demonstration of 1 May 2011, and had a semi-structured interview with a social worker and a student counsellor. This additional information will provide us with more information about the operation of schools, of various types, in Macao.

Supplementary Information: News Clippings, Observations, and Personal Communications

In addition to giving the general background and specific insights into the operation of the Macao education system, we have sought to supplement this with information from additional sources to provide us with some sense of public views on education in Macao. Macao Daily is the major local newspaper in Macao; its readership covers over 95% of the reading population. Given Macao Daily's extensive reach, this book relies on it and some other local publications to provide an overview of how educational issues are viewed and discussed by the general public in Macao.

The second author is an expert in the history of education in Macao and originally from Macao. The first author is a sociologist researching into educational inequality, originally from Hong Kong. This combination of views and analyses will, we argue, provide readers with both insider and outsider perspectives on educational issues in Macao. The first author taught between 2009 and 2013 at the Faculty of Education, University of Macau, where she met the second author. Making use of the second author's social connections in Macao and also getting his practical assistance, the first author has been able to access study targets of various types: getting documents (such as teacher manuals), and recruiting students and teachers, of various types, for different research projects discussed above. But for such assistance from the second author, these four research projects would have been impossible. Working at the University of Macau also allowed the first author to have casual chats and even conduct informal interviews with students and teachers on relevant topics. The first author taught both undergraduate programmes (i.e., those for prospective teachers) and PGDE programmes (i.e., those for in-service teachers). And the courses she taught were called 'Introduction to Education,' 'Sociology of Education' and 'Youth Culture'. In teaching these courses, the first author asked students to share their educational experiences and to assess the applicability of various sociological concepts in education to Macao. The conversations and informal interviews that followed amounted to an informal analysis of the operation of the Macao education system and also the current practices of teachers and schools in Macao. All this information will also be quoted where necessary to illustrate our points and/or substantiate our arguments.

Limitations of the Data

As much as we do our best to make use of a wide range of data, from various sources, our data have their limitations. Readers should be cautious in interpreting analyses undertaken in the book. And let us make explicit at the outset the limitations of the data used in this book.

As already mentioned, we draw on official statistics to sketch an overview of education in Macao. The Education and Youth Bureau (DSEJ) has provided an abundance of statistics on different sectors of education in Macao, which has indeed been of great help. However, as with many other official datasets, the categories found in official data provided by the DSEJ are not necessarily congruent with what is needed for the arguments developed by this book. Indeed, some DSEJ categories can even be shown to become inconsistent over time. Therefore, it is difficult to rely completely on official data to support our arguments at all times or to accurately document trends over time.

Apart from official statistics, we draw on clippings of a major local newspaper and material from a number of research projects. Newspaper clippings can be used to reflect some public views on issues concerned; yet, the coverage of the newspaper and our selection could well be biased due to the particular concerns of this book. The research projects follow specific research agenda and are not designed to study random or representative samples of their respective study targets; and respondents of different projects are asked to look retrospectively. Statistical representativeness and reliability could therefore be an issue. Nevertheless, by taking such a wide variety of information into account, we are confident that this information can give us a valid account of what is going on in the education system in Macao. With that said, we do not seek to imply that this is the only possible interpretation of educational data in Macao. Rather, our analyses remain tentative, while opening up new lines of inquiry for further discussion, which is absolutely crucial for improving the education system in Macao.

Organization of the Book

In this book we have tried to be as comprehensive as possible; including information from as many sources as we could to give readers a better idea about the operation of the Macao education system. Thus, in order to facilitate a systematic discussion of educational issues in Macao, we shall first provide readers with a general contextual background for ongoing educational issues. Chapter 2 will describe the major characteristics, given the colonial legacy of Macao, of its existing system of basic education. Chapter 3 will provide an overview of the recent economic, political, and social development of Macao, including the changes in the education system. Chapter 4 will highlight the major developments in education in Macao before the 1999 handover. These chapters will enable readers to understand that the education system in Macao is essentially a system of private schools and that the freedom of schools to run themselves in their own style has been guaranteed by the Basic Law in Macao since its 1999 handover to the PRC.

Following this general background, we shall then discuss different aspects of the operation of the existing Macao education system: its legal foundation (i.e., education laws), its institutions (i.e., schools), its frontline practitioners (i.e., teachers), and its recipients (i.e., students). Chapter 5 will discuss the legal foundation of the provision of education in Macao; in particular the two major laws governing education: the fundamental law of non-tertiary education set in 1991 (11/91/M) and the 2006 law to replace it (9/2006). The provision of free and compulsory education for all school-age children is secured by this legal foundation; but the Macao SAR government has not been able to monitor the operation of the education system as closely as it has planned, especially at school level. Chapter 6 will examine the management of schools in Macao, focusing on the relationships with their teaching staff and students. Despite increased government monitoring, many schools continue to run as they did in the colonial Portuguese era, with complete freedom on matters of curriculum, formal examinations, teacher hiring and retention, and even student selection (and disqualification). This historical independence explains the diversity of types of school management in Macao, which in turn, we argue, constitutes a major reason for the dubious professionalism of teachers and for the questionable quality of education that students receive. This then brings us to the discussion of the practices of teachers (the frontline practitioners of education), and the schooling experiences of students (the recipients of education).

Chapter 7 will examine how the work and market situations of teachers in Macao have implications for their professionalism and also their professional development. Chapter 8 will look into the schooling experiences of students and seek to make sense of a low completion rate (i.e., a high dropout rate) and a high grade-retention rate in Macao.

This brings us to the concluding part of the book. Having looked into different aspects of education in Macao, highlighting challenges facing the Macao education system in particular and Macao in general, Chapter 10 will summarize what has been done and what needs be done if the Macao education system is to change. We discuss what we can learn from the case of Macao, with particular reference to the neoliberal discourse dominant in many industrial-capitalist societies that supports the privatization of education. Drawing on Macao's experience, we argue that a system of private schools without effective state regulation or governance does not necessarily bring in quality education. Therefore, we urge educators to reconsider the values of competition, choice, efficiency and effectiveness as defined by neoliberalism, and the validity of the promise of quality education offered by this discourse.

Chapter 2

THE CHARACTERISTICS OF THE EDUCATION SYSTEM IN CONTEMPORARY MACAO

This book is mainly concerned with identifying challenges to the basic education system of Macao by examining such issues as high grade retention and low completion (in other words, the number of drop-outs). To this end, we need to understand the historical and social context in which these issues occur. This chapter and the next provide exactly this background/contextual information. In this chapter, we will briefly describe the immediate context of the basic (non-tertiary) education system in Macao, focusing on the most relevant statistics from official and legal documents. Then, we will describe the basic education system in some detail, highlighting different stages that each school-age child has to go through in order to qualify. And finally, we shall summarize the major characteristics of this education system.

AN OVERVIEW OF BASIC EDUCATION IN CONTEMPORARY MACAO

According to the official definition by the Education and Youth Affairs Bureau (DSEJ), which is responsible for non-tertiary education in Macao, basic education in Macao is now classified into two types: formal and continuing education. "Formal" education includes kindergarten, primary education, secondary education, and special education. "Continuing" education includes recurrent education (basic education for those who either left school without qualifications or never attended school at all; usually conducted in evening schools, as mentioned in Chapter 1), family education, community education, and occupational training. Vocational and technical education, which may be implemented as part of formal education or recurrent education, is only offered at senior secondary school level. In this chapter, unless otherwise stated, our discussion relies heavily on the most recent official statistics posted on the DSEJ website.

During the 2011/2012 school year, 5,284 teachers were working in the basic education sector. 73,425 students were receiving a basic education; 70,719 receiving it in what is classified as "formal" education. (The distribution of students by different types of education is shown in Table 2.1.) Of these students in formal education, 560 (0.8%) were enrolled in institutions for children with special educational needs; 11,787 (16.1%) were in kindergarten; 22,646 (30.8%) in primary school; and 35,726 (48.7%) in secondary school. 1,601 of these secondary-school students were also receiving vocational or technical education. Some 2,706 students (3.7%) were receiving basic education in the form of recurrent education, including 216 primary school pupils and 2,490 secondary school students.

Table 2.1. Distribution of students by types of education in Macao during the 2011/2012 school year

Form of education	Number of students	Proportion of students
Formal education:	70,719	96.3%
Kindergarten (pre-primary education)	11,787	16.1%
Primary education	22,646	30.8%
Secondary education	35,726	48.7%
Special education	560	0.8%
Recurrent education:	2,706	3.7%
Primary education	216	0.3%
Secondary education	2,490	3.4%
Total	73,425	100.0%

Source: the website of DSEJ:
http://portal.dsej.gov.mo/webdsejspace/internet/category/learner/Inter_main_page.jsp?id=22748.

The education system in Macao comprises public and private schools. As a legacy of Macao's colonial past, most schools are still private, with about 95% of students studying in private schools. For example, during the

2011/2012 school year, there were 78 licensed schools in Macao (the license determining which type or types of education each school offers, from primary to recurrent education). Of this number, 11 were public schools with the remaining 67 being private schools. Of the total number of schools, 66 offered formal education only, 3 offered recurrent education only, and 9 offered both formal and recurrent education. During the 2012/2013 school year, nearly 96% of students studied in private schools. Leaving aside special education, only 5% of students (at every educational level) were in public schools, as shown in Table 2.2.

Table 2.2. Distribution of students in formal education by form of education in Macao during the 2012/2013 school year

Formal education	Number (Proportion) of students in public schools	Number (Proportion) of students in private schools	Total (Proportion)
Kindergarten (pre-primary)	340 (2.7%)	12,329 (97.3%)	12,669 (100%)
Primary education	514 (2.3%)	21,905 (97.7%)	22,419 (100%)
Secondary education (including vocational education)	1,804 (5.0%)	34,341 (95.0%)	36,145 (100%)
Special education	290 (49.8%)	292 (50.2%)	582 (100%)
Total	2,948 (4.1%)	68,867 (95.9%)	71,815 (100%)

Source: the website of DSEJ: http://portal.dsej.gov.mo/webdsejspace/internet/category/learner/Inter_main_page.jsp?id=8525.

The Current Basic Education System

The current system of basic education in Macao might be described in essence as publicly funded but privately run. All public schools and most private schools – getting subsidies from the Macao SAR government – provide children aged between 5 and 15 with a compulsory basic education. At present, every child in Macao is entitled to fifteen years of free and compulsory basic education. Since 2006, the following educational model has become standard for all school-age children in Macao: three years of pre-primary education, six years of primary education, and six years of secondary education (i.e., three years of junior secondary education and three years of senior secondary education). Table 2.3 sketches out the overall system: it indicates the different stages of basic education, the duration of each stage, in addition to the legal upper age limit set for three stages. The legal upper age limit for those in primary education is 15; for those in junior secondary education it is 18; while for those in senior secondary education it is 21. If a student leaves a particular strand of education and returns to it beyond the legal age limit, they must do so in the form of "recurrent education".

Table 2.3. The existing system of basic (non-tertiary) education in Macao

Educational stage (duration)	Age range	Upper age limit
Pre-primary education (3 years)	3-5 years old	NA
Primary education (6 years)	6-11 years old	15 years old
Junior secondary education (3 years)	12-15 years old	18 years old
Senior secondary education (3 years)	16-18 years old	21 years old

As mentioned at the outset, the system of education in Macao is basically founded on private schools. There are 11 public schools, but the remaining private schools are run by a variety of organizations. In the next two chapters, we shall discuss in more detail the impact of Macao's history on the differentiation of school types, but for the present purpose, we shall differentiate schools according to their respective educational missions. Three major types of schools provide a basic education in Macao: public schools; schools run by traditional organizations (such as trading organizations, neighbourhood associations, lineage associations, and the Federation of Labour Union); and schools organized by the Catholic Church. The remaining nine schools in Macao are categorised as "other" schools, a residual category. Seven of these are Protestant schools, one is a Buddhist school, and one is an international school.

The educational focus of government or public schools can also be seen as a colonial legacy: they have gradually become aligned to the Macao SAR government, but bear traces of their missions from the Portuguese colonial period. Thus, schools run by traditional organizations are pro-PRC. They make it explicit that the teaching of patriotism is part of their educational agenda. Similarly, schools organized by the Catholic Church make it clear that their educational mission is to transmit the teaching of Catholicism. The educational missions of other schools are likewise set by their respective funding organizations. With similar educational missions, schools of each type design very similar school regulations for their students and treat their teaching staff in a similar way, as will be discussed in the chapters on students and teachers respectively. Table 2.4 displays the distribution of primary and secondary schools by school type.

Table 2.4. Distribution of schools in Macao by school type

School type	Number of primary schools	Proportion of primary schools	Number of secondary schools	Proportion of secondary schools
Government schools	5	7.81%	3	6.98%
Schools run by traditional organizations	23	35.94%	15	34.88%
Schools organized by the Catholic Church	23	35.94%	16	37.21%
Other schools	13	20.31%	9	20.93%
Total	64	100.00%	43	100.00%

Concentrating on private schools, their management and the quality of education they offer varies tremendously. As will be discussed in the next chapter, one of the legacies of colonialism is that there was, and still is, not much coordination among schools in Macao. In fact, under colonial rule, schools funded by different organizations adopted completely different educational models; with a standardised model only coming into effect in 2006.

Given this basic lack of coordination, there is no standardization across private schools in regard to curriculum and pedagogy (as summarized in Table 2.5). Students are taught in at least one of the following languages: Chinese, English or Portuguese. In the absence of a common curriculum, schools are free to adopt one of their own choices. Public schools tend to adopt a Portuguese curriculum; Catholic schools tend to adopt a Taiwanese curriculum; and, private schools run by traditional organisations tend to adopt a PRC curriculum. Still others adopt the Hong Kong curriculum.

Similarly, at the level of individual educational subjects, schools will take their syllabus and textbooks from Portugal, Taiwan, China and Hong Kong respectively – aiming to prepare their students for university entrance examinations in those countries. This does not necessarily disadvantage students, because, in the absence of a centralised exam board in Macao, students need only pass the subjects supported by their respective schools to qualify for a high-school diploma.

Table 2.5. A summary of schools by their teaching language and curriculum

	Public schools	Schools run by traditional organizations	Catholic schools	Other schools
Teaching language	Chinese/ Portuguese	Chinese/English/ Chinese and English	Chinese/English/ Chinese and English	Chinese/English/ Chinese and English
Curriculum	Portuguese	The PRC	Taiwanese	Hong Kong

This phenomenon of schools choosing their own curriculum and setting their own examinations is true at all levels of basic education in Macao. There is no common academic standard at any stage. One consequence of this is that obtaining a qualification at one stage does not guarantee students a place in the following stage of the education system.

In other words, the education system in Macao is stratified. Kindergartens prepare their students for primary schools run by the same or connected organizations; primary schools, in turn, essentially prepare students for promotion to secondary schools run by the same or connected organizations; and, secondary schools prepare students for entrance examinations set by pre-designated universities in different regions. In consequence, if a student changes schools mid-stream, they are often required to read an entirely different curriculum. Similarly, it is not unheard of for students to study several different curriculums at once in order to maximise their chances at entrance examinations set by different universities. In short, while there is strong vertical integration between kindergartens and schools run by the same organisations, horizontal integration between schools of the same type is very weak.

Characteristics of the Modern Education System

As mentioned, the current system of basic education in Macao can be defined as publicly funded but privately run: it is a system of predominantly private schools funded by the Macao SAR government. Basic education is compulsory between the ages of five and fifteen, and free to students at the point of delivery. Parents have a legal obligation to enroll their children in school every year, while the government and educational institutions are similarly obliged to ensure that school-age children complete compulsory education. Since 2007, compulsory education has become free for a period of fifteen years. This comprises three years of kindergarten (pre-primary education), six years of primary education, three years of junior secondary education, and three years of senior secondary education.

The Macao SAR government provides this free basic education by two means: directly, through running public schools; and indirectly, through allocating funds to private schools that join the free education network, and by allocating tuition fee subsidies to students attending private schools outside the free education network. The exact amounts of subsidies provided are summarized in Table 2.6.

Table 2.6. Free Education Subsidies and Tuition Fee Subsidies in the 2011/2012 school year

Educational stage	Free education subsidies (MOP)	Tuition fee subsidies (MOP)
Kindergarten	570,000 per class	12,000 per student
Primary education	600,000 per class	13,000 per student
Junior secondary education	770,000 per class	14,000 per student
Senior secondary education	870,000 per class	14,000 per student

Note for free education subsidies:

If the class size is smaller than the stipulated lower limit, subsidy is calculated as follows: (subsidy amount shown above ÷ stipulated lower limit) x actual number of students.

Source: the website of DSEJ:

http://portal.dsej.gov.mo/webdsejspace/internet/category/learner/Inter_main_page.jsp?id=22753.

In the 2011/2012 school year, the SAR government increased funding overall by raising free education subsidies in every section. The subsidies for each class of senior secondary education, junior secondary education, primary education, and kindergartens were raised to MOP 870,000 (35-45 pupils per class),[1] MOP 770,000 (35-45 pupils per class), MOP 600,000 (25-35 pupils per class), and MOP 570,000 (25-35 pupils per class), respectively. Similarly, the SAR government also raised the tuition fee subsidies in the 2011/2012 school year. The subsidies for kindergarten pupils were increased to MOP 12,000 per head, for primary school pupils to MOP 13,000 per head, and for secondary school pupils to MOP 14,000 per head.

In addition, the SAR government has been making an effort to reduce class size and promote small-class teaching. This effort began in the 2007/2008 school year and initially covered the first year of pre-school education. It was subsequently expanded to cover other school years. In 2011, the upper limit to the number of pupils in the fourth year of primary education was extended into the sixth year, speeding up implementation of small-class teaching. The SAR government also offer textbook allowances. In the 2011/2012 school year the SAR government increased the textbook allowances for secondary and primary school pupils to MOP 1,700 per head, while each kindergarten pupil received an allowance of MOP 1,500.

In summary, after the 1999 handover to PRC, the Macao SAR government has been allocating more and more funding and resources to basic education. Nevertheless, the underlying structure of the education system remains one of private schools. When the Portuguese colonial government established the Fundamental Law of Non-tertiary Education (the Law 11/91/M) in 1991, the aim was to regain the power to monitor the operation of private schools and recentralize the operation of the education system. However, this initiative followed a long period of colonial neglect; in order to convince various schooling organizations to agree to be monitored, the Portuguese government resorted to using financial subsidies as a kind of incentive. The financial situation of the colonial government was such that these subsidies were not immediately attractive to private schools. In the end, in finalizing Law 11/91/M, the Portuguese colonial government had to make concessions to major schooling organizations such as the Catholic Church that preserved the scholastic and managerial autonomy of private schools. That autonomy was then rubber-stamped by the Macao Basic Law.

The result has been that private schools both receive more government funding than ever before while retaining their historic management styles. This independence extends into nearly every aspect of their organization: from their academic calendars (different numbers of semesters beginning and ending on very different dates) to their teaching schedules (including taking holidays

[1] Approximately, 1 US dollar = 8 MOP.

without consideration of national holidays). More importantly, private schools enjoy autonomy in managing their teaching staff, controlling students, and designing the curriculum. One of the consequences of this freedom is that schools can have independent, and often very different, criteria for the hiring, monitoring and firing of their teaching staff. Even the Private Legal Frame of 2012 guarantees that private schools have complete freedom to choose teachers to fill institution-specific needs (rather than according to a curriculum) and to offer differing remuneration packages to teachers depending on their academic backgrounds. Equally, private schools can draw up their own teacher manuals to regulate teachers' performance, and can fire teachers without giving reasons as long as they comply with the basic labour laws of Macao. Such autonomy has tremendous implications for the professionalism of teachers in Macao, as will be discussed in Chapter 7.

This autonomy of private schools extends into their management of students, including the recruitment, regulation, and disqualification of students. Private schools can design their own criteria for student admission and set their own tuition fees, together with other types of fees. They can adopt a curriculum of their liking and set their own school regulations and academic standards (including the criteria for grade retention) in order to discipline students and regulate their academic performances overall. They can essentially disqualify or expel their students wherever they see fit. Such autonomy has tremendous implications for the quality of education in Macao, as will be discussed in Chapter 8.

SUMMARY

Basic education in Macao is now compulsory for children aged between five and fifteen and it is free for fifteen years for school-age children. As a result of Macao's colonial legacy, the education system remains a system of private schools; or more precisely, it is publicly funded but privately run. Because the Basic Law guarantees private schools complete autonomy with regard to curriculum and management, there are basically no professional requirements for teacher recruitment or the assessment of teachers' professionalism; nor is there a common curriculum and standardized examinations across schools for students. Government-run (public) schools provide education to only 5% of the student population, but are well resourced by the government. For example, teachers in government schools will tend to receive a much higher salary than their counterparts in the private system.

Teachers' pay in the private system tends to vary hugely across (and even within) schools. The gap in security of tenure and remuneration between public and private teachers greatly influences the quality of education in Macao. The Private Legal Frame, passed in March 2012, was intended to provide a core standard of education to pupils in private schools, but the standard of teaching remains variable. Teachers can still be hired and fired at the whim of school principals; with teachers being monitored by different standards in different schools. These factors pose serious obstacles to the overall professionalism of teachers in Macao. Without a common curriculum, it is unclear what should be taught to Macao students; and, without standardized examinations, it is unclear what academic standards Macao students are expected to achieve by the time they complete basic education. As a result of all these challenges, it remains unclear what kind of people Macao want to nurture and what qualities Macao want its people to acquire. But no education system can be understood in a vacuum. This is why the next chapter looks at the wider social context: that of the history and society of Macao.

Chapter 3

MACAO TODAY

Where the previous chapter sought to provide readers with an overview of the immediate context of the basic education system in Macao, this chapter seeks to enable readers to understand the wider context of our discussion: that of Macao itself. Macao is a former Portuguese colony and is now a tourist city in Southeast Asia (Gunn, 1996; cf. Porter, 1996). It was returned to the People's Republic of China (PRC) in 1999 and since then has been a special administrative region of the PRC. Macao stands on the western side of the Pearl River Delta, with Hong Kong to the east, and is bordered to the north by Guangdong Province. Macao is a small place. Its 29.5 square kilometres consist of three parts: the Macao Peninsula and the islands of Taipa and Coloane. The islands are now connected to the peninsula by a landfill development known as the Cotai Strip. According to the most recent official statistics – the Macao Census of 2012 – the population of Macao is around 500,000. Macao is essentially a Chinese society. 90% of its population is ethnically Chinese. According to the 2006 Population By-Census, 42.5% of the residents were born in Macao, 47% on mainland China (of whom 74.1% were born in Guangdong and 15.2% in Fujian), and 3.7% in Hong Kong.

Transforming from a Portuguese colony to a special administrative region of the PRC, Macao has witnessed tremendous changes over the last decade. In particular, its economic development and education system have changed rapidly in line with a new political consensus. Our discussion of educational issues in Macao is necessarily engaged with this rapidly changing social context. This chapter provides a very brief account of the major social and political changes in Macao since the Second World War, especially since the 1999 handover. We shall focus particularly on major changes in three domains: economics, politics and education. The last decade in particular has seen massive changes in all three sectors (e.g., Wong et al., 2007; Wang et al., 2009; Cheung et al., 2014). Let us first take a look at Macao's economic development.

MACAO'S ECONOMY

As the folk saying goes, Macao has changed from a small fishing village to an international tourist city. Unlike many developed industrial countries in the West, Macao is not an industrial society; it is rather a society dominated by tourism, holiday resorts and in particular the gambling industry (repackaged as "the gaming industry") (Lam and Scott 2011). The GDP of Macao and its GDP per capita has increased over the years, with some ups and downs, as summarized in Table 3.1. This chapter aims to summarize the characteristics of Macao's economic performance in different periods.

There are no reliable official statistics or information showing the distribution of the working population by industry in the early days of Macao, but it is widely acknowledged that by the early twentieth century most of the local Chinese population were employed in three labour-intensive industries: producing matchsticks, fireworks and incense sticks. Industrialization appeared to arrive in Macao in the 1970s, with the establishment of various industrial processing plants, but the industrial boom did not last very long (e.g., a collection of essays in Cheung et al. 2011). This partly explains the change in categorizations of work in successive Macao censuses. After the brief industrial boom of the 1970s, many Hong Kong entrepreneurs moved their factories to Macao, taking advantage both of cheaper rent and lower labour costs, and the favourable export quotas set for "developing regions" such as Macao. These factories were largely focused on labour-intensive light industries, such as textiles, garments and toy manufacture. There was also a small agricultural sector, as indicated in Table 3.2, but over half the population was employed in the secondary (processing) sector. This domination of the secondary sector weakened as the 1980s became the 1990s, with manufacturing eventually growing to employ over 30% of the working population.

Table 3.1. GDP of Macao (expenditure-based) and its GDP per capita, 1984-2012

Year	GDP (in billion MOP)	GDP per capita (in MOP)
1984	10.00	35250
1985	10.29	35506
1986	11.57	39082
1987	14.97	48772
1988	17.65	55842
1989	20.91	64309
1990	25.10	74941
1991	29.05	82608
1992	38.03	102532
1993	43.64	113657
1994	48.65	122615
1995	54.47	133074
1996	55.29	133194
1997	55.55	133130
1998	51.64	122280
1999	49.39	115550
2000	50.58	117470
2001	51.13	117777
2002	54.80	125013
2003	62.34	140064
2004	80.35	175843
2005	92.14	193516
2006	113.70	227710
2007	141.90	269900
2008	161.60	294377
2009	165.58	304211
2010	226.94	422656
2011	295.05	537103
2012	348.22	611930

Source: http://www.dsec.gov.mo. Figures for the years 1984-2009 are from the same file. Figures for the years 2010-2012 are from a separate file.

The decline of the secondary sector in Macao from the 1970s into the 80s was largely due to the PRC's 1978 'Open Door Policy', which saw many industries in Hong Kong move north to the mainland. This trend was mirrored in Macao: many factories run by Hong Kong entrepreneurs in Macao also started to move to China. As indicated in Table 3.3, the secondary sector of Macao shrank from employing more than half of the working population

(53.67%) in 1981 to employing little more than one-fifth of the working population (22.2%) in 2006.

Table 3.2. Distribution of the working population in Macao, 1981, 1991

Industry	% of the working population in 1981	% of the working population in 1991
Agriculture and fishery	6.04	1.39
Refinery industry	0.06	---
Processing industry	45.02	---
Mining	---	0.03
Manufacturing	---	32.34
Electricity, gas, water supplies	0.70	0.63
Construction	7.95	7.84
Wholesale and retail trade, hotels and restaurants	18.47	22.18
Transports, storage and communications	4.62	4.85
Finances and insurance (and banking in 1991)	1.75	4.79
Services (and social welfare in 1991)	15.39	25.96
Total	100.00	100.01

Source: Macao SAR statistics and census service.

Table 3.3. Distribution of the labour force in the three economic sectors, 1981-2006

Sector	1981	1991	1996	2001	2006
Primary sector	6.10%	1.42%	1.40%	1.10%	0.80%
Secondary sector	53.67%	40.81%	27.40%	27.60%	22.20%
Tertiary sector	40.23%	57.78%	71.10%	71.30%	77.00%
Total	100.00%	100.01%	99.90%	100.00%	100.00%

Source: Macao SAR statistics and census service.

Table 3.4 shows the minimal presence of manufacturing in Macao today: in 2011, it employed less than 4% of the working population. In summary, it is debatable whether meaningful industrialization ever took place in Macao; if it did, it lasted less than a decade. The withdrawal of Hong Kong-run factories in Macao has limited the availability of job options to many people in Macao – especially poorly educated immigrants from mainland China.

In contrast to the secondary sector, the tertiary sector of Macao has expanded since the 1980s from employing about 40% of the working population in 1981 to 77% in 2006. Table 3.2 above shows a particularly fast development in the service and financial industries between 1981 and 1991. The proportion of the working population in the service industry increased from 15.39% in 1981 to 25.96% in 1991, with the financial and banking sector expanding from 1.75% of the working population to 4.79%.

It would be a mistake to perceive the economic development of Macao as one of linear growth. As Table 3.1 indicates, the economy of Macao underperformed in certain years leading up to the 1999 handover. In the face of this underperformance, the public debated hotly whether to expand Macao's gambling industry, with a particular point of contention being whether to open up gambling licenses to competitive tender when the central monopoly ended in 2002.

The Macao SAR government eventually liberalised its gambling regime, allowing three companies a gambling license, and the first new casino was completed in 2004. The rapid expansion of Macao's tertiary sector since then has been built not on services or finance and insurance, but on gambling. Table 3.4 compares the distribution of the working population by industry between 2001 and 2011.

Table 3.4. Distribution of the working population by industry in Macao, 2001-2011

Industry	% of the working population in 2001	% of the working population in 2011
Recreational, cultural, gaming and other services	11.6	25.6
Hotels, restaurants and similar activities	11.4	14.0
Wholesale and retail trade	15.1	12.5
Construction	7.2	8.2
Public administration and social security	8.3	7.9
Real estate and business activities	5.6	7.6
Education, health and social welfare	6.6	6.9
Transport, storage and communications	7.4	5.2
Domestic work	2.2	5.0
Manufacturing	19.8	3.4
Financial services	3.1	2.9
Others	1.7	0.9
Total	100.0	100.1

Source: http://www.dsec.gov.mo

Table 3.5. Employment by industry, the number of the population (in 1000 in the upper row) and the proportion of the total working population (in the upper row), selected years between 1998 and 2012

Industry	1999	2002	2005	2008	2011	2012
Recreational, cultural, gaming and other services	19.3 10.9%	23.5 12.7%	40.8 19.0%	77.4 27.1%	82.0 28.4%	89.5 29.6%
Hotels, restaurants and similar activities	21.0 11.9%	23.6 12.8%	24.9 11.6%	40.8 14.3%	46.1 16.0%	53.0 17.5%
Wholesale and retail trade	30.4 17.2%	31.4 17.0%	35.3 16.4%	38.9 13.6%	43.4 15.0%	42.3 14.0%
Construction	16.2 9.2%	15.3 8.3%	22.9 10.7%	37.6 13.2%	28.2 9.8%	32.3 10.7%
Public administration and social security	16.3 9.2%	17.4 9.4%	18.8 8.7%	19.4 6.8%	23.0 8.0%	25.1 8.3%
Real estate and business activities	9.3 5.3%	11.0 6.0%	14.3 6.7%	23.4 8.2%	28.0 9.7%	24.3 8.0%
Transport, storage and communications	14.5 8.2%	13.1 7.1%	14.8 6.9%	15.6 5.5%	16.0 5.5%	16.0 5.3%
Manufacturing	42.7 24.2%	42.0 22.7%	35.3 16.4%	24.3 8.5%	12.8 4.4%	10.3 3.4%
Financial intermediation	5.8 3.3%	6.3 3.4%	6.6 3.1%	7.3 2.6%	8.1 2.8%	8.2 2.7%
Electricity, gas and water supply	1.3 0.7%	1.2 0.6%	1.2 0.6%	0.8 0.3%	1.3 0.4%	1.5 0.5%
Total	176.6 100.1%	184.8 100.0%	214.9 100.1%	285.5 100.1%	288.9 100.0%	302.5 100.0%

Source: http://www.dsec.gov.mo.

It makes it clear that the proportion of the working population employed in recreational, cultural, gaming and other services more than doubled between 2001 and 2011, from 11.6% to 25.6%. Looking more closely at the distribution of the working population, in Table 3.4, we also see a clear expansion of the hotel and restaurant sectors, which are to a large extent dependent on the gaming industry.

As Table 3.1 above showed, Macao has generally enjoyed strong economic growth since the 1980s, with a particular peak following the liberalisation of gambling licenses. The GDP of Macao more than doubled from about 80 billion in 2004 to over 160 billion in 2009. It then nearly tripled to about 220 billion by 2010, and more than quadrupled to over 340 billion in 2012. From that point to the present day, the gambling industry has accounted for more than 80% of Macao's GDP.

The rapid expansion of the gambling industry has also boosted tourism and attracted a lot of foreign investments, leading to the expansion of the hotel and restaurant industry and the retail industry. Table 3.5 summarizes the changes in the development of different major industries over the past fifteen years, showing both the total number of the population working in each industry and that number as proportion of the total working population.

What is remarkable about Tables 3.4 and 3.5 is that the recent economic expansion of Macao is essentially a result of the boom of the gaming industry (i.e., other industries actually seem to decline gradually over time), and that about a quarter (25.6% in 2011) of the working population makes a living from the gaming industry. This proportion is predicted to rise still further soon. Put simply, the gaming industry and associated trades are the lifeblood of present day Macao. Further development along these lines could pose serious challenge not only to development of education in Macao, but to the democratization of the society as a whole. This takes us into an overview of the development of Macao's political domain.

Political Domain

In contrast to its rapid economic development over the last decade, the political development of Macao has not been particularly remarkable since its handover to the PRC. Macao's political culture is characterised by its focus on local civic organizations (Chan, 2011; Hung and Ip, 2014). This characteristic is to a large extent a function of Macao's colonial history, whereby the more or less ineffectual Portuguese government was contrasted with a strong civil society made up of ethnic Chinese. Given the day-to-day remoteness of the colonial government, the Chinese had to rely on themselves to solve problems in almost every aspect of their lives, including education (as will be discussed in the next section). More specifically, the Chinese in Macao became accustomed to forming various types of civic organizations to take care of needs that central government had overlooked. This political culture of local civic organizations has continued since the 1999 handover.

To reemphasize an earlier point, 90% of Macao's population is ethnic Chinese and Macao can for that reason be considered essentially a Chinese society. During the colonial period, the Portuguese and Chinese populations essentially led their own lives (Gunn, 1996). Their social circles were broadly segregated, with each group largely living in totally different areas of Macao. It was further believed that the Portuguese ruled Macao through the Chinese elites, in particular Chinese merchants. In short, the colonial Portuguese government was accountable to Lisbon taking care of the Portuguese and their offspring in Macao, but did not interfere with the lives of the local Chinese. After the 1911 revolution in China some Chinese intellectuals came to Macao (as will be discussed further in the following section), such that the influence of the KuoMinTang (KMT) became significant in education in Macao. After end of the civil war between the Communists and the KMT in 1949, the Communists came to power and established the PRC, with the KMT retreating to Taiwan. Despite this geographical divide, the two camps – the pro-KMT blue camp and the pro-PRC red camp – competed for political influences among the local Chinese in Macao. The colonial Portuguese government did not side with any of them but witnessed their political competition.

This uneasy state of equilibrium between the Portuguese and the Chinese (and between the pro-PRC camp and the pro-KMT camp) broke down in 1966 because of the incidence of '12.3.' This incident resulted from a dispute between the local Chinese and the Portuguese colonial government over the building of a local school for the Chinese in Taipa in November 1966. After a few months' struggle in which the PRC's influence became strongly apparent in Macao, the Portuguese colonial government finally had to apologize to the public for their maltreatment of the local Chinese. After this, the pro-KMT camp's influence in Macao declined, while the Portuguese colonial administration gradually became a lame-duck government, incapable of governing Macao effectively. It was in this political vacuum that the ethnic Chinese in Macao began to form various types of civic organizations to take care of their different needs, including education. This practice of self-reliance continued after the 1999 handover. As of 2009, there are 4,409 registered civic organizations in Macao, covering commerce, labour, different professions, culture, the academy, charities, the community, neighbourhood, family, socializing, sports, etc. (Chan, 2011). Table 3.6 provides some examples of this. Crucially, without the historic competition provided by the pro-KMT camp, many civic organizations were now avowedly pro-PRC.

Table 3.6. Examples of civic organizations taking care of various aspects of social needs

Civic organization	Targets served
Macau Tung Sin Tong Charitable Society	All residents in Macao
Kiang Wu Hospital Charitable Association	All residents in Macao
Macao Federation of Trade Unions	Workers
União Geral das Associações dos Moradores de Macau	Civilians
The Macao Chamber of Commerce	Merchants
Macao New Chinese Youth Association	The youth
The Chinese Educators Association of Macao	Schools and teachers
Association of Chinese Students — Macau	Students
Associação dos Trabalhadores da Função Pública de Macau	Civil servants
Macao Association of Building Contractors and Developers	Developers
The Macau Association of Banks	Banks

Basic education in Macao has largely been provided by private schools. Given the strong civil society in Macao under colonial rule, these private schools were largely run by civic organizations of the type described above. Three civic organizations in particular are active in the field of education in Macao: The Chinese Educators Association of Macao, the Union of Catholic Schools of Macau, and Associação Educativa da Função Pública de Macau.

Before the handover, these civic organizations represented the local Chinese in negotiations with the Portuguese colonial government to safeguard the interests of the local Chinese population. However, after the 1999 handover, when the Macao SAR government came to power under the rubric of 'one country two systems' and 'Macao people rule Macao,' the negotiating roles of such civic organizations became less clear, particularly with regard to the overall democratization of Macao under the SAR government. The heads of civic organisations in Macao tend to be drawn from the ethnic Chinese elite, a pattern observed in educational organizations whose heads tend to be school principals. This may lead to an overrepresentation of managerial interests in negotiations with government, and a consequent underrepresentation of the interests of teachers and students. One example of this has been the debate over the last decade of legal protection for teachers' pay, benefits and rights (which will be discussed in detail in the forthcoming chapter on teachers). As with many things in modern Macao, the imbalance of voices from different stakeholders in Macao's education system is partly a result of its development from colonial to Chinese rule. This brings us to a discussion of the educational sector itself.

Education Sector

As we have seen, under Portuguese colonial rule, the Portuguese and the Chinese lived in separate areas and the local Chinese developed their own system of social services through the establishment of civic organisations. Under colonial rule, Macao had government-run schools, but they were meant to provide education for the children of the Portuguese in Macao (Bray, 1992). As we have also seen, the employment structure of colonial Macao was rather basic for the local Chinese population: not many jobs required any specific formal qualifications. As a result, demand for even a basic education was not very strong. Where basic education was provided, it was done at the behest of the local civic society. Private schools for Chinese students were funded and managed by a variety of organizations, including religious institutions, trading associations, and civil organizations such as neighbourhood associations, lineage associations, or the Federation of Labour Union (Clayton, 2009).

Schooling in colonial Macao was neither free nor compulsory, and each civic organisation responsible for a school ran it according to its own educational mission. Private schools of this type could therefore design their own educational models, with no coordination across schools or educational institutions (cf. Choi and Koo, 2001).

Table 3.7. Different educational models in Macao before the 1999 handover

Model	Description
A modified Portugal model (with reference to the Portugal model in the 1980s): 4+2+3+2+1	4 years of primary education + 2 years of preparatory secondary education 3 years of junior education 2 years of senior education + 1 year of matriculation
A modified PRC model (with reference to the model of the 1980s): 6+5	6 years of primary education 5 years of secondary education
A modified Taiwanese model in the 1980s: 6+3+3	6 years of primary education 3 years of junior education 3 years of senior education
A modified Hong Kong model in the 1980s: 6+5+1	6 years of primary education 5 years of secondary education 1 year of matriculation

Table 3.7 shows the four educational models operational in Macao during the colonial period, each consisting of primary and secondary education of different lengths for a different numbers of years. There was a modified Portugal model (4+2+3+2+1), a modified PRC model (6+5), a modified Taiwanese model (6+3+3), and a modified Hong Kong model (6+5+1).

Despite their different educational models, two broad types of private schools came to dominate the scene: religious schools and non-religious schools. Religious schools were almost invariably run by the Catholic Church (although there were some Protestant and Buddhist schools): their mission was essentially to spread a particular religious belief in Macao through education. Schools in the non-religious sector were basically managed and organized by individuals, trading organizations, or civil organizations. As mentioned above, before 1966, non-religious private schools were a battleground for the pro-PRC red camp and the pro-KMT blue camp for overall political influence in Macao through education. After the '12.3 incident' in 1966, blue-camp schools run by pro-KMT organizations withdrew from Macao; and from then onwards, private schools of the non-religious type were organized by so-called "traditional" organizations and were essentially pro-PRC. From this period on, the two major pillars of basic education in Macao have been Catholic schools and schools run by these "traditional" pro-PRC groups.

The Portuguese revolution of 1974 led to a recognition in Portugal that if sovereignty in Macao belonged anywhere, it belonged with China. Curiously, it was only after this recognition that the Portuguese colonial government began to exert itself to leave a historical mark on Macao (cf. Bray, 1992). The government decided to allocate more resources education in Macao, with the specific goal of spreading the Portuguese language. In 1977, to this end, the colonial government passed its first education act to provide subsidies to local private schools to aid the provision of basic education for the local Chinese. In order to receive these subsidies, however, schools were required to teach the Portuguese language.

The subsidies included exempting schools from property tax on their grounds and avenues. In 1984, a further act was passed, providing an array of help to teachers, even exempting them from income tax. It is unclear how successful these acts were in spreading Portuguese through Macao, but vastly more resources were now available for education, and, above all, the general public was now involved in a discussion about the provision of free basic education for all school-age children. Finally, in 1991, the first comprehensive education law was passed: Law 11/91/M.

This law is widely accepted as having been rushed and leaving much room for improvement. Following two further government decrees (Decree 29/95/M and Decree 34/97/M, establishing free education for seven and ten years respectively); basic education finally became freely available on the eve of the 1999 handover.

Since the handover, the Macao SAR government has sought to improve the provision of education in Macao. As a result of the increased GDP resulting from the liberalisation of Macao's gambling laws in 2002 and the growth of the gaming sector, much public debate focused on improving education, and in particular replacing Law 11/91/M with a more comprehensive framework. This framework – Law 9/2006 – came into force in 2006.

Table 3.8 summarizes expenditure on education between 2002 and 2009. Expenditure on education in total has nearly tripled from MOP 1,684 million to MOP 4,372 million, while expenditure on basic education has increased from MOP 1,007 million to MOP 2,763 million respectively. The total invested in every student has likewise tripled in absolute terms: from MOP 13,083 in 2002 to MOP 35,794 in 2009. However, expenditure on education accounted for only 13% total government expenditure of the SAR in 2009 and only about 2-3% of Macao's GDP.

The provision of education in Macao has been improved and education itself has become more and more institutionalized (fifteen years of free compulsory education was guaranteed by law in 2007). But such improvements do not change the fact that most schools are private schools and about 95% of students attend them.

Table 2.4 in Chapter 2 summarized the distribution of all primary and secondary schools by type in modern Macao, showing that the majority of schools are either run by the Catholic Church or traditional organizations (cf. Bray and Koo, 2004). There are very few government schools in comparison, and an even smaller number of schools run by other organizations.

Table 3.9 shows that, in fact, the number of students has been in decline over the last decade, dropping from 97,000 in 2003/2004 to about 74,000 in 2009/2010. This fall in number has not changed the distribution of students in private versus other schools, as indicated in Tables 3.9 and 3.10.

Tables 3.9 and 3.10 also show that more and more private schools have joined the free education network, thereby getting subsidies from the government. A greater number of school-age children are therefore enjoying a free basic education at private schools inside the school network subsidized by the SAR government, although the proportion of students outside the school net remains around 14-16%.

Table 3.8. Financial indicators of education, 2002-2009

Financial indicator of education	2002	2003	2004	2005	2006	2007	2008	2009
Expenditure on education (in million MOP)	1684	1839	1907	2219	2611	3028	3704	4372
Proportion of total expenditure on education (in %)	16.3	15.2	14.0	14.1	14.9	16.2	14.0	13.0
Expenditure on basic education (in million MOP)	1007	1083	1056	1207	1539	1912	2347	2763
Proportion of total expenditure on basic education (in %)	9.8	8.9	7.8	7.7	8.8	10.2	8.9	8.2
Proportion of GDP on education (in %)	3.1	2.9	2.3	2.4	2.3	2.1	2.3	2.6
Proportion of GDP on basic education (in %)	1.8	1.7	1.3	1.3	1.4	1.3	1.5	1.7
Expenditure on each student receiving basic education (in MOP)	NA	NA	NA	13083	17454	22819	29586	35794

Source: Chan, 2010, p.225 Tables 4.1 and 4.2.

Apart from providing a free basic education for school-age children, more resources have also been invested to improve the quality of teachers and to decrease the teacher-student ratio. The qualification standards needed by teachers have increased tremendously over the last two decades.

In the late 1980s, around 70% of teachers did not have a degree or an educational diploma and thus were disqualified from teaching (Wong, 1991), as indicated in Table 3.11. In contrast, by 2007 about 80% of teachers in Macao had a bachelor's degree or a post-graduate degree and were thus qualified to teach, as indicated in Table 3.12.

Table 3.9. Distribution of students (in number) by school in government schools and private schools, 2003-2010

School type	2003/04	2004/05	2005/06	2006/07	2007/08	2008/09	2009/10
Government school	4958	4456	4166	3904	3384	3175	3007
Private schools	92799	90383	87447	83707	77439	73234	70819
Inside school net	75671	76804	74351	71202	65445	61635	59038
Outside school net	17128	13579	13096	12505	11994	11599	11781
Total	97757	94839	91613	87611	80823	76409	73826

Source: Chan, 2010, p.201 Table 1.22.

Table 3.10. Distribution of students (in proportion) by school in government schools and private schools, 2003-2010

School type	2003/04	2004/05	2005/06	2006/07	2007/08	2008/09	2009/10
Government school	5.07%	4.70%	4.55%	4.46%	4.19%	4.16%	4.07%
Private schools	94.93%	95.30%	95.45%	95.54%	95.81%	95.84%	95.93%
Inside school net	77.41%	80.98%	81.16%	81.27%	80.97%	80.66%	79.97%
Outside school net	17.52%	14.32%	14.29%	14.27%	14.84%	15.18%	15.96%
Total	100.00%	100.00%	100.00%	100.00%	100.00%	100.00%	100.00%

Calculation based on Table 3.9.

Table 3.11. Qualification of teachers in the late 1980s

Qualification	Number of teachers surveyed	Proportion
Junior secondary education	28	6.6%
Senior secondary education	260	61.3%
Post-secondary diploma (including an education diploma)	101	23.8%
Bachelor's degree	35	8.3%
Total	424	100.0%

Source: Wong, 1991: p.183 Table 1.

With so much investment in education, the Macao SAR government has sought to improve the quality of education, reflected in changes in the average class size and teacher-student ratio over the last decade. Table 3.13 shows that the average number of students in each class decreased greatly between 1999/2000 and 2009/2010 at every level: from about 38 to about 25 at pre-primary level; from about 45 to about 30 at primary level; from about 45 to about 35 at junior secondary level; and, from about 39 to about 34 at senior secondary level. In addition, the government has spent more to employ additional subject-specific teachers, with the aim of decreasing the overall teacher-student ratio. Table 3.14 shows this ratio decreasing markedly between 1999/2000 and 2009/2010 at every level: from about 1:30 to about 1:17 at pre-primary level; from about 1:31 to about 1:16 at primary level; and from about 1:23 to about 1:16 at secondary level. This reduction in average class size and teacher-student ratio is intended to enable teachers to take better care of each student and provide each student with a better quality of teaching.

Table 3.12. Qualification of teachers in 2007

Qualification	Number of teachers surveyed	Proportion
Secondary education or below	54	6.08%
Post-secondary diploma	126	14.19%
Associate degree	62	6.98%
Bachelor's degree	497	55.97%
Post-graduate degree	126	14.19%
Others	23	2.59%
Total	888	100.00%

Source: the website of the DSEJ on the qualification of teachers.

Table 3.13. Average class size by educational level, 1999-2010

Level	1999-00	2000-01	2001-02	2002-03	2003-04	2004-05	2005-06	2006-07	2007-08	2008-09	2009-10
Pre-primary	37.9	37.0	35.0	33.2	32.3	30.8	29.7	27.0	25.9	25.0	24.9
Primary	45.2	42.6	41.8	39.5	37.3	36.6	35.6	34.2	32.6	31.0	29.7
Junior secondary	45.3	45.0	45.1	44.9	44.3	43.6	42.3	39.8	37.9	35.5	34.7
Senior secondary	39.2	40.1	40.5	40.8	41.2	41.1	40.8	39.5	37.8	35.0	34.3

(Source: Chan, 2010, p.228 Table 4.7)

Table 3.14. Teacher-student ratio by educational level, 1999-2010

Level	1999-00	2000-01	2001-02	2002-03	2003-04	2004-05	2005-06	2006-07	2007-08	2008-09	2009-10
Pre-primary	1:30.2	1:29.9	1:28.9	1:27.1	1:26.0	1:23.8	1:22.9	1:19.2	1:18.1	1:17.6	1:17.2
Primary	1:30.8	1:29.2	1:28.2	1:26.5	1:25.2	1:24.1	1:22.6	1:20.9	1:18.9	1:17.3	1:16.1
secondary	1:23.2	1:23.6	1:23.5	1:23.8	1:22.9	1:22.0	1:21.2	1:20.3	1:19.0	1:17.1	1:16.2

(Source: Chan, 2010, p.228 Table 4.7)

To summarize, at present every student in Macao is entitled to a fifteen-year free and compulsory basic education. In addition, the SAR government also seeks to standardize the practices of private schools and to regain governance of the education sector from disaggregated education providers. At the same time, however, the Basic Law guarantees private schools in Macao the freedom to run themselves in their own style. Consequently, the attempts of the Macao SAR government to change old practices or to standardize diverse practices have been resisted by schools in the name of academic freedom. Granted, the government has made some progress. Instead of having a multi-track system of schools (e.g., Bray, 1992), since 2006 the educational model of all schools in Macao has been standardized. Regardless of which schools they attend, students in Macao now have six years of primary education, three years of junior secondary education, and three years of senior education (6+3+3). This has not however altered the fact that private schools in Macao are free to design their own curriculum and assessments, nor the overall makeup of the education sector in Macao, which continues to be dominated by private schools.

To return to an earlier point, there is still no common curriculum and public/standardized examinations in Macao. There are also no legally required entrance requirements for teachers. Without a common curriculum, schools in Macao are free to follow a PRC, Taiwanese or Hong Kong curriculum using corresponding textbooks. Without a standardized examination, students sit individual school examinations at the end of six-year secondary education. In order to study further, students in Macao have to sit the examinations required by different tertiary institutions. This risks overloading students with preparation for different examinations. In spite of the passing of The Private Legal Frame' in March 2012, schools are still free to hire teachers to their own liking, without reference to accepted qualifications. It therefore remains unclear what level of teaching quality Macao aims to provide for school-age children. Put simply, despite investing a lot in education, the Macao SAR government still cannot effectively monitor or assess the quality of education provided by different schools. In subsequent chapters, we shall seek to highlight pressing educational issues in relation to schools, teachers, and students in Macao. The next chapter provides a brief account of education in Macao before the 1999 handover, to enable readers to understand what makes it so difficult for the Macao SAR government to standardize some important practices of private schools in Macao.

Chapter 4

EDUCATION IN MACAO BEFORE 1999

In order to get at the essence of the issues affecting Macao's education system today, it is useful to have a wider historical perspective. The aim of this chapter is to describe the development of education in Macao prior to the 1999 handover to the PRC. To this end, we shall highlight various issues and critical turning points from the establishment of the PRC in 1911 up to 1999.[1]

Using the Second World War as a demarcation point, we identify six broad periods in two eras, as listed in Table 4.1. For the era before the Second World War, we differentiate three periods according to critical developments in education in Macao: before 1911; between 1911 and 1936; and from 1936 to 1945. To summarise this pre-war period: before 1911, education for the local Chinese in Macao was almost entirely neglected by the Portuguese colonial government. From 1911 to 1936, education for the Chinese population was usually provided by religious organizations from the West and some Chinese charity agencies. Chinese intellectuals and private schools came to Macao in large numbers after 1937, when the Sino-Japanese war broke out. This period could be considered a boom era for education in Macao.

For the era after the Second World War, we also identify three periods: 1945 to 1966, 1967 to 1990, and 1991 to 1999. The conclusion of the Second World War led to civil war between the Communists and the ruling KMT on mainland China. The KMT government lost power in 1949 and fled to Taiwan, with the Communists taking power and establishing the PRC. In outlying territories such as Macao, however, the KMT and the PRC continued to compete for political influence. The Communists set up the federation of

[1] The information listed in Chapter is from a collection of books on the history of Macao edited by Ng et al. (2008) and from book published by DSEJ (1994).

workers, which in turn ran schools for the grassroots in Macao. Pro-KMT "blue camp" schools could be differentiated from pro-PRC red-camp schools in Macao.

Table 4.1. An overview of the development of education for the local Chinese in Macao before 1999

Period	Turning point/Characteristics
The era before the Second World War	
Before 1911	The colonial neglect of education for the education of the local Chinese
1911-1936	The rise of private schools
1937-1945	The flood in of elite schools
The era after the Second World War	
1945-1966	The coexistence of different school models
1967-1990	The withdrawal of the pro-KMT blue camp schools, paving the way for the free provision of a basic education
1991-1999	The improvement of the provision of basic education for the Chinese

Nevertheless, the 1966 '12.3 incident' changed this educational ecology. After the incident, pro-KMT schools withdrew from Macao, one after another. This meant that from 1967 onwards schools organized by traditional organizations were all essentially pro-PRC. Towards the end of Portuguese rule, the colonial government decided to invest in education for the Chinese in Macao, passing the law 11/77/M to provide subsidies of various kinds to schooling organizations and teachers. This started the first major public debate in Macao about the provision of free basic education for the Chinese. While preparing to cede Macao to Chinese rule, the Portuguese colonial government finally established its first Fundamental Law of non-tertiary education in 1991. This is a milestone in the development of education in Macao and serves as the basis for further development. For the time being, however, let us turn to the development of education in Macao before the Second World War.

Education in Macao before the Second World War

From the first appearance of the Portuguese in Macao, the Portuguese and Chinese populations of the territory lived in different areas and were thus effectively segregated. When the Portuguese finally took Macao as a formal "colony" in the late nineteenth century, this segregation continued more or less as before. In the sphere of education, this meant that the Portuguese looked after their own children but essentially neglected the education of the local Chinese population. This state of affairs continued until 1977 (as will be discussed below).

Education for the Chinese before 1911 was provided by a variety of religious organizations, especially the Catholic Church, some Chinese charity agencies, and some Chinese private schools in the most traditional form (學塾). A private school in the most traditional form refers to a school privately run by an intellectual teaching his students the Chinese classics; and the name of the school is usually the name of the intellectual. For example, prior to 1911 in Macao there private schools called Tao Rui-yun private school (陶瑞雲學塾), Xiao Lian-fang private school (蕭蓮舫學塾), Kong Hou-tian private school (孔厚田學塾), and Lin Lao-ku private school (林老虎學塾). Each of them was named after its founder and sole employee.

The situation whereby personal private schools took care of basic education of the Chinese remained even after the 1911 revolution, when the KMT government came into power. But some progressive Chinese intellectuals such as Chen Tzu-pao (陳子褒) and Liang Yue-ming (梁彥明) not only ran their own private schools but also made significant contributions to promote the provision of basic education for the Chinese in Macao by setting up private schools in a modernized form. Chen Tzu-pao private school (子褒學塾), for instance, had been founded in 1899, but was modernized in 1912 to promote education for women and children. Similarly, Liang Yue-ming's Chongshih private school (崇實書塾) became Chongshih school (崇實學校) with a modernized curriculum. The number of such schools mushroomed in a short space of time. Aside from these well-known educators, some Chinese merchants set up an English school in 1914; and many private primary schools in a modern form also came into being. To Ying primary school (陶英小學) and Lai Kwan primary school (勵群小學) were set up in 1923, while Yuet Wah secondary school (粵華中學) and Hou Kong primary school (濠江小學) were set up in 1928 and 1932 respectively. These schools were accorded official status by the KMT government, with the KMT accepting the registration of Chinese private schools, leading to the foundation of the Chinese Educators Association of Macao (中華教育會) in 1920.

In addition to progressive intellectuals, formal education was also provided in Macao by some religious organizations. Many schools were set up by the Roman Catholic Church. The most famous of these was the School of Immaculate Conception (聖母無原罪學校) set up in 1906, later renamed as

Don Bosco primary school (鮑思高學校) and finally as Salesian School (慈幼學校). Escola Dom Joao Paulino (聖善學校) was set up in 1911 with some others, including those run by other Christian denominations, established around the same period.

When the Sino-Japanese war broke out in 1937, many schools in Guangdong province moved to Macao to escape from the war. According to the available contemporary documents, those schools included Zong-li Gu-xiang Memorial Middle School (總理故鄉紀念中學), Zhi-xin Middle School (執信中學), Xie-he Girls' High School (協和女子中學), Jie-fang Girls' Middle School (潔芳女子中學), Pui Ying Middle School (培英中學), Si-si Middle School (思思中學), Giao-zhong Middle School (教忠中學), and others. This trend accelerated when the Second World War broke out in 1941, with Macao's neutrality attracting more and more elite schools. Examples during this period include Lingnan Middle School (嶺南中學), Chong Tak Secondary (中德中學), and Pui Ching Middle School (培正中學). This influx of elite schools to Macao laid the foundation of the post-war influence of the KMT in education in Macao. This general influx of educators and schools served to boost Macao's education system in the run-up to and during the war. But this situation did not last. When the war ended in 1945, many Guangdong schools and their teaching staff, including the many well-known educators, decided to return to mainland China. Due to a post-war economic slump, and a drastic drop in population that decreased the numbers of students, many schools in Macao went from a period of relative plenty to one of scarcity. The very survival of schooling in Macao hung in the balance.

While Macao had gone through a sort of education boom before and during the war years, with many famous educators and elite schools arriving there, the situation did not survive the post-war settlement. In particular, it did not change the amount of resources generally available to private schools. As a result, the pay of teachers in Macao remained very low. The result was that the quality of teaching was indifferent at best. Given the general background of colonial neglect, Macao could certainly take pride in a strong civil society where a variety of organizations were so willing to shoulder the provision of basic education for the local Chinese. However, willingness did not result in adequate resourcing, nor in the professionalization of teaching staff. This historical conundrum is the root of many perennial problems found in the subsequent development of education in Macao.

Education in Macao after the Second World War

Right after the end of the Second World War in 1945 came the Chinese civil war between the ruling KMT and the Communists. When, in 1949, the KMT was ousted and fled to Taiwan, the Communists came to power and established the People's Republic of China. Given the international politics of the time, the PRC refrained from demanding that Britain and Portugal to return such territories as Hong Kong and Macao immediately to Chinese rule. So the Portuguese remained in Macao, as did the colonial government's focus on the provision of education to the Portuguese community, with the local Chinese making their own way through the educational support of various civic and religious organisations. The post-war retreat of elite schools to Taiwan and mainland China left a vacuum at the heart of education in Macao, which a great many pro-PRC organizations moved to fill – the idea being to exert political influence through schooling. Macao was different to other historically Chinese territories in that it retained a significant pro-KMT population. Many pro-KMT schools continued to run in Macao, in direct competition to the new pro-Communist schools. The third pillar of education in Macao in this period was religious organizations, which usually meant the Roman Catholic Church. The three major providers of education in Macao maintained a wary equilibrium until 1966, when the '12.3 Incident' took place. The violence and civil disobedience of this period effectively left the Portuguese colonial government powerless and forced pro-KMT schools and organizations out of Macao altogether. This allowed pro-PRC schools to make even further inroads to the mainstream, reinforcing pro-PRC tendencies in existing traditional organizations. In the absence of the KMT, the three main pillars of education in Macao today are the government schools, Catholic schools, and schools run by traditional organizations (pro-PRC).

Ironically, it was precisely at the point that the Portuguese colonial government began to lose control of Macao that it began to take a sincere interest in the educational well-being of the local Chinese population. The Portuguese revolution of 1974 led the Portuguese to adopt a gradual decolonization policy and to promote democracy in general. It wanted to return Macao to the PRC. Given the global geopolitical climate of the time, the PRC declined to take back Macao but made it clear that a handover should occur in due course. Realizing their days in Macao were numbered, the Portuguese colonial government wanted to leave a mark before returning Macao to Chinese rule. This led to the first conscious effort to provide for the education of the local Chinese population. The Chinese population was at first suspicious about such a move. Mr. Sin (冼為鏗), a retired teacher interviewed by the second author, recalled that as a high official of the Chinese Educators Association of Macao, he had to argue with private schools about accepting Portuguese assistance at all. In the end, the first education law concerning all people of Macao, including the Chinese, was passed in 1977: Law 11/77/M. From then on, the Portuguese colonial government invested limited resources in education for the Chinese. In 1984, after some amendments to this law, the Portuguese colonial government released subsidies to teachers working in private schools in Macao for the first time. Mr. Yau (邱子維), another retired teacher interviewed by the second author, expressed his surprise about and appreciation for the financial assistance: 'I found it unbelievably pleasant receiving the subsidies from the Portuguese colonial government for the first time. Working as a teacher for more than twenty years, I got not a penny from the Portuguese; I was pleased to get the living allowance of MOP 600. In the 1970s, in general the pay of most teachers was around MOP 2000, an additional MOP 600 was a big help!'

Signing the Sino-Luso joint declaration in April 1987, the Portuguese colonial government made its first formal efforts to prepare for a handover of Macao to the PRC. By this time, in addition to having supplied free basic education to all in Macao and subsidies for teachers in private schools, it had also belatedly sought the introduction of Portuguese as a teaching language in Macao. This was a carefully scripted deal: private schools could receive additional subsidies and financial support from the colonial government, but only if they taught Portuguese, and only if they agreed to give up some of their historic legal independence and submitted to a centralized curriculum and standardized testing. Private schools responded that diversity in educational models did not contradict the provision of free basic education, and refused to teach Portuguese or to standardize the curriculum and testing. The colonial government severely criticized this decision, but years of neglect had left them in a weakened position with regard to local civil society in Macao. In the end, the colonial government had to provide a free basic education, without pre-conditions.

While the efforts of the colonial government surely accelerated the uptake in provision of free basic education throughout Macao, that government's failure to standardize the curriculum or examinations had cast a long shadow over education in Macao ever since. The first comprehensive education law was enacted in 1991: the Fundamental Law of Non-tertiary Education (the law 11/91/M). A rushed piece of legislation, aiming to cover all sectors and types of schools, it subsequently needed to be bolstered by supplementary decrees over the next few years. In fact, it was only on the eve of Macao's handover to the PRC that free and compulsory basic education was finalized. In 1995, basic education was decreed to last seven years (one year of pre-primary education and six years of primary education). In 1997, this was extended to ten years (one year pre-school, six years of primary education, and three years of junior secondary education). As mentioned in Chapter 3, a fifteen-year basic education has become free and compulsory in 2007 (consisting of three years pre-school, six years of primary education, and six years of secondary education). What was different about the post-1991 era compared to what had come before is that these changes all took place against the background of wide public debate.

The first major debate was about how many years of free education should be provided. The Portuguese government had only so much money to spend on education, so it could initially make only a very basic education freely available to school-age children. The public was solidly of the opinion that free provision of basic education should gradually be extended to secondary education. When this provision was extended to ten years in 1997, a debate began about extending compulsory education to twelve years, and how much coverage should be given either to pre-primary education or senior secondary education. In the end, it was decided to extend free education to fifteen years, covering every stage of basic education.

This debate was accompanied by another about the form government subsidies should take when it came to aiding private schools. Should the subsidies come in the form of vouchers for individual students, or in the form a voluntary free education network that would distribute funds centrally? The sticking point about vouchers was that vouchers would make it very difficult for some schools to budget for the forthcoming year pro-actively, so in the end the free education network was preferred. However, as discussed in Chapter 2, this has effectively led to a two-track approach to government subsidies: with the schools receiving one form of subsidy if they are part of the free education network, and students receiving a tuition subsidy if their schools are not part of the network.

In terms of the speed with which education provision grew in Macao between 1991 and 1999, this era could be seen as a milestone in the development of education in Macao. But some issues remain unresolved. For example, while the SAR government has been providing greater resources and subsidies to private schools, there is no evidence of a corresponding improvement in either teacher pay or teacher performance. It also seems that there is no adequate centralized means to monitor how private schools spend their subsidies, let alone to ensure that it is being used in the classroom or to improve the quality of teachers they seek to recruit. To sum up, despite a great improvement in the provision of a basic education in Macao, it seems unlikely that this increase in provision has been accompanied by an increase in the quality of education.

Concluding Remarks

The education of the local Chinese population in Macao was essentially neglected under colonial rule. After the 1911 revolution in China, progressive Chinese intellectuals came to Macao and began teaching in their own self-run schools. Schools in the modern style began to appear in Macao in the years between the Sino-Japanese war and the end of the Second World War. However, when these personal schools began to return to mainland China after 1949, the vacuum was filled by private schools run by traditional organizations and funded by a strong civic society among the local Chinese in Macao. These schools were financially constrained by the lack of central government subsidy and the quality of the education they provided was doubtful. These are historical features that still to some extent mark the provision of education in Macao today: while there is near-universal coverage in basic education, the quality of teaching and instruction varies tremendously. Even in the 1970s and 1980s, when big efforts were made to reform education, some reforms were strongly resisted by private schools. The strength of this resistance was effectively given force of law by the first Fundamental Law of Non-Tertiary Education (Law 11/91/M), which failed to centralize control of the education system or provide a standard curriculum or assessments for private schools. Private schools continue to act and manage themselves with near complete autonomy. This scenario poses obstacles and serious challenges to further reform in Macao, as will be seen in Chapters 6 to 8. Let us first discuss the legal foundation of education in Macao.

Chapter 5

LEGAL FOUNDATION OF EDUCATION IN MACAO

If there was no centralization or standardization to education in Macao, this did not necessarily mean that there was no regulation. The first Fundamental Law of Non-tertiary Education in Macao (11/91/M) was established by the colonial Portuguese government in 1991. In its design, it sought to be flexible enough to incorporate differences across schools, with each of the previously described models of management and education legally recognized and justified. According to Basic Law no. 121, the Macao SAR government is now required to formulate its own education policy. In 2003, the SAR government introduced proposals to reform the first education law (Chan, 2010). After three years' consultation, the new Fundamental Law of Non-tertiary Education (Law 9/2006) was passed in December 2006. In this chapter, we discuss these two educational laws, which provide a legal foundation for the provision of basic education for everyone in Macao.[1]

LAW 11/91/M

This law effectively brought into existence a consistent and comprehensive education system for all. As discussed in Chapter 4, education for the local Chinese population in Macao was largely neglected by Macao's colonial government, with the burden being shouldered by voluntary traditional organizations in the community. By law, these establishments were considered 'private schools' and as such were not entitled to resources from

[1] The laws and decrees mentioned in this Chapter are summarized in Chan and Ieong (2012).

government for their teachers and students. This opened up a gap between public and private schools in Macao; one which persists, with a few differences, to this day. The gap broadly consists in the relative quality and quantity of school facilities, the professional quality of teachers (and teaching), and the overall quality of education received by students.

In 1974, the Portuguese revolution ended with Portugal becoming a democratic republic. Portugal recognised that under the tenets of democratic republicanism it could no longer treat Macao as a colony. However, because the People's Republic of China declined to take back Macao at the time, the Portuguese government in Macao engaged in a progressive, if belated, attempt to respond to the broad societal needs of Macao. To this end, the government passed Law 11/77/M and began to provide central resources for private schools. Although the resources allocated were quite scarce, this can still be seen as a landmark for the development of education in Macao. For instance, Law 11/77/M allowed registered non-profit private schools to enjoy tax exemptions and to receive minimal subsidies. The tax exemptions were broadly focused on property taxes, while the government subsidies were based on class size, the language of instruction (Portuguese was favoured), and school rents. Law 11/77/M was followed in 1984 by a decree (65/84/M), which saw an increase in support for private schools in the form of teaching aids, school facilities and resources for continued teacher training and development. Yet support of all kinds remained minimal in real teams. It was also perhaps a question of too little, too late: in almost a century of colonial rule, these were the first real interventions into education by the colonial government. And even these important reforms were imposed rather than discussed, which meant that the first real public debate about free universal education did not take place till after the Luso-Chinese declaration of 1987: the pact in which Portugal formally agreed to return Macao to Chinese rule on 20 December 1999.

Over the decade that the handover was planned, educators in Macao made a strong case to the colonial government that resources were needed for the basic education of the local Chinese. The argument was founded on the idea that the youth of Macao needed to be nurtured in order to fulfil the goal of 'Macao ruled by Macao people'. The original request from educators in 1985 was for a nine-year basic education. Additional requests were for increased subsidies to private schools, improved remuneration and terms for school teachers, and for financial assistance. The colonial government, keen to leave a lasting mark before handing control to the PRC, acceded to these demands, but set a number of conditions of its own: the stipulation that this education should be free to children and their parents, the standardization of the educational model throughout Macao, and a guarantee to promote the Portuguese language. This last request was taken particularly poorly by Macao's largely Chinese civil society, but there were also protests on the grounds that different educational models were an established part of Macao's history and society. In the end, of the colonial government's proposals, only the idea of free basic education was accepted. Even that took until 1991 to be established, and its legal implementation only began in 1995. The initial seven years of compulsory education were extended to ten in 1997 (via Law 34/97/M), with a fifteen-year period of free and compulsory basic education coming into force in 2007. Let us now look at the social concerns that underlie this particular progress in educational law.

Concerns Underlying the Law

Macao's colonial government primarily intended free and compulsory education to be a vehicle for the teaching of Portuguese in schools. However, there were nine broad issues the lawmakers were seeking to address: defining the education system in Macao, establishing the rights of Macao residents to education, formulating a new education system, building up school networks, defining what an educational system was, establishing the language of instruction, establishing and administering educational funds, making a clear organizational chart for every school, and developing the curriculum. Let us address these issues one by one.

1. Defining the Macao Education System

The Law seeks to provide the legal framework for the Macao education system. The Law defines itself as the foundation on which the Macao education system should be based, and that it seeks to establish the fundamental rights of Macao residents with regard to education, to work towards the personal development of students, and thereby to ensure social progress and the eventual democratization of Macao.

The Law states clearly that all public and private institutions can serve as providers of education but that the coordinating power lies in the government. The Law applies to all educational institutions in Macao and seeks to monitor their organization and regulate their operation. The Law seeks to be flexible enough to incorporate a diversity of educational institutions, allowing that schools in particular and the system as a whole can retain local specificity while building and maintaining connections to international counterparts.

Given the unique history of Macao, this Law seeks to preserve and strengthen the cultural heritage of Macao, and to respect the democracy and diversity of Macao society. In nurturing students, the Macao education system places a lot of emphasis on students' respect for others and engagement in open dialogues and free exchanges of opinions. This, in turn, means to enhance students' ability to think critically and enable students to engage with social affairs. Apart from this, the Law seeks to enable students' personal development in the hope that students will become independent, responsible, autonomous, cooperative, and sociable residents, and that they will be able to forge harmonious relationships with people from all around the world.

Given the unique social development of Macao, the Law seeks to make sure that the potential of Macao residents will be developed to the full, so that they will take up posts that match their interests and abilities, and will eventually contribute to the progress of the society. It also seeks to ensure the provision of vocational training for changing societal needs, while securing the right of Macao residents to a second chance for education (if they have dropped out of school) and for continuing education.

2. Establishing the Rights of Macao Residents to Education

The Law states clearly the right to education of Macao residents. Regardless of race, religious affiliation, political beliefs or ideologies, every Macao resident is entitled to education. Teachers and learners alike should be freed from educational contents with particular philosophical, aesthetic, political, ideological, or religious underpinnings. The Law furthermore states clearly that the Education Bureau has to make ensure that each Macao resident has an equal opportunity to assess their education and to become educationally successful. Through counselling and/or educational assistance, an equal opportunity for assessing and receiving education is created for all Macao residents. In addition, a series of welfare measures such as subsidies for higher education, tuition allowances for non-higher education, allowances for meals, and allowances for educational utilities are provided for students with financial difficulties so as to ensure that all students genuinely enjoy an equal opportunity for education.

Given the historic neglect of education under the Portuguese colonial government, this last issue is of particular importance. For the bulk of the colonial period, government schools only taught Portuguese children, with very few ethnic Chinese children receiving any sort of formal education at all.

The Law therefore provides a legal guarantee of a limited free education for all residents of Macao. For the first time, equality of opportunity was enshrined in education law in Macao.

3. Formulating a New Education System

The Law seeks to establish a comprehensive education system that includes every stage from pre-school education to higher education, across a number of different sectors and styles of educational institution: including vocational education, special needs education and adult education. The core of the formal education system comprises nursery education, pre-primary education (kindergartens, etc.), primary education, a two-part secondary education system, higher education – as well as vocational, adult, and special needs education. There are specific legal requirements for each of the seven domains:

1. Childhood Education (for 1-2 Years)

Family activities are taken as supplementary; the emphasis is on the cooperation between the family and school.

The goals of childhood education are eightfold: aiding family education; enabling the physical and intellectual development of children and their emotional balance; developing children's ability to manage their mother tongue, especially their ability to comprehend and articulate orally; developing children's ethical concept and their interests and creativity; establishing children's habits concerning their hygiene and health; exposing children to different social environments; and, identifying maladaptive children so that timely appropriate assistance or guidance can be provided.

Childhood education is regarded as an integral domain taken up by professional pre-primary educators. The targets of childhood education are children aged 3 or 4 years old. It is required that eligible children should become 3 years old by 31 December of the year of application. At this stage, no assessments for social promotion should be based on academic knowledge.

2. Basic Education (for 10 Years: 1 Year of Pre-Primary Education, 6 Years of Primary Education, and 3 Years of Junior Secondary Education)

Everyone has the right to basic education. Different stages of basic education should be free (in practice, this has happened gradually). Free basic education is provided by government schools, and by private schools with government aid. Free education covers the tuition fees and fees related to registration and certification of those studying in any such school, and also the allowances for tuition fees of those studying in private schools ineligible for government aid.

One-year pre-primary education aims to achieve the same goals as childhood education. In addition, it aims to teach to students the basics of literacy and numeracy and develop their command of the language of instruction. The entrance to pre-primary education is not dependent on assessment. Students should be aged 5 by 31 December of the year of application. Pre-primary education is conducted by professional pre-primary educators. Assessments for checking academic progress should be standardized for social promotion.

There are ten main goals in the provision of the six-year primary education. First, it aims to improve students' ability of verbal expression. Second, it seeks to develop students' reading and writing abilities in the language of their choice while enabling them to learn a second language. Third, it aims to enable students to master basic concepts in understanding arithmetic, nature and society. Fourth, it seeks to enhance the physical and spiritual growth of students through the teaching of craftwork and drama and the promotion of art education. Fifth, it seeks to teach students the current situation in Macao and enhance their personal development. Sixth, it provides students with moral and civic education. Seventh, it teaches students hygiene and develops their health habits. Eighth, it seeks to ensure that students with special learning needs can develop their potentials to the full and in every aspect. Ninth, it nurtures students to think critically and independently so that they can make sense of problems in their own lives and Macao society as a whole. Tenth, it seeks to provide instructional techniques and facilities for students so that they can continue to learn by their own initiative. Students should complete pre-primary education before their entrance to the first year of primary education. There may be exemptions for students aged above 5. Schools should decide whether to set up assessment mechanisms in recruitment under such circumstance; but the assessment standard should not exceed the pre-primary level. Students should be aged 6 by 31 December of the year of application. The upper age limit for primary education is 15. In completing a primary education, students are eligible for a corresponding diploma.

There are two stages in secondary education: junior secondary education and senior secondary education. Students who pass the primary level of education are allowed to enter the junior level of secondary education. There are four goals in the provision of three-year junior secondary education. First, it aims to guide students to learn systematically in the domains of humanity, art, nature, sports, and technology. Second, it seeks to strengthen the moral and civic education of students. Third, it aims to enhance the academic growth of students and their development so that they can make appropriate decisions on further studies and employment. Fourth, it should seek to create a learning environment where students' choices are respected in order that they may make decisions for their future education and careers.

3. Secondary Education (for 5-6 Years: 3 Years of Junior Secondary Education, As Covered in Basic Education, and 2-3 Years of Senior Secondary Education)

The section on junior secondary education is the same as above.

The duration of senior secondary education is two to three years. There are six goals in the provision of senior secondary education. First, through systematic learning, observation, and practice, senior secondary education aims to strengthen students' knowledge in the domains of humanity, art, and technology. Second, it seeks to enhance the intellectual and physical development of students and cultivate their curiosity in sciences and new matters, so that they can apply what they have learnt at school in their lives. Third, it aims to provide students with required knowledge for higher education if they choose to study further, or with relevant vocational training if they choose to enter the labour market. Fourth, it seeks to enable students to keep pace with the development of the labour market and the society as a whole so that they can understand better social issues and actively participate in social affairs. Fifth, through participation, it seeks to arouse students' interests in local and international issues. Sixth, it seeks to strengthen the moral and civic education of students.

4. Higher Education

This educational stage is monitored by a separate set of laws and decrees.

5. Special Education

In view of the principle of equal opportunity for education, special education seeks to provide education for people with special needs in the following aspects: mental, emotional, muscular and physical, social, communicative, and sundry other needs.

Special education refers to activities arranged for students with special needs and arrangements designed for their families, teachers, and associates. Special education provides tailor-made instructional arrangements, designing special plans for students with special needs, so that the students can integrate in society with regard to education and employment. In order to create opportunities for education for people with special needs, the DSEJ gives priority to private organizations seeking to provide special education.

6. Adult Education

Adult education targets adults who exceed the age limit for a variety of formal educational levels. It seeks to facilitate the educational growth of adults and enable them to develop their potential. Adult education is considered to be supplementary to formal education.

Adult education particularly targets problems of literacy. It seeks to provide opportunities for education for adults who have never received or have not completed formal education. In this way, it seeks to enhance participation in civil education and cultural activities. Adult education consists both of continuing education (i.e., adults returning to school to complete their formal education) as well as voluntary informal education in the form of night classes, etc.

Adult education is meant to consist of a set of flexible learning plans tailor-made for people with a variety of needs, awarding a qualification equivalent to its counterpart in formal education. It is recommended that adult education should take place in non-office hours. The DSEJ is further recommended to give priority to supporting private organizations that seek to provide or develop adult education.

7. Vocational Education

Vocational education is meant to be complementary to formal education, with the emphasis on preparing students for certain lines of work. In addition, vocational education seeks to assist the overall developmental needs of Macao by training semi-qualified technicians or functionaries so that they become experts.

There are two modes of vocational education: vocational training and vocational and technical education. Vocational training refers to training that meets the needs of the labour market and continuing economic development. It therefore seeks to provide a basic level of training: pre-service training, professional training, in-service training, and training that facilitates occupational changes (in cases where economic development has made some traditional roles insecure). Vocational training can be provided by public or private vocational training organizations, or by formal schools. It should be open to teenagers or adults who have completed primary education.

Certificates of achievement are awarded to all who successfully complete the vocational courses.

Vocational and technical education seeks to nurture experts or technicians of a middle level of professional qualifications and provide them with the basic knowledge and skills required for a particular profession. Vocational and technical education training can be provided by public or private vocational schools and formal schools. The duration of these courses should generally be about two to three years, with the final year of such education focused on apprenticeship. Courses in vocational and technical education are equivalent to the secondary level of formal education. Vocational and technical education is a type of formal education; its graduates are qualified to get into institutions offering higher education, especially polytechnics. After completing vocational and technical education satisfactorily, people are eligible for corresponding certificates. Those who get into polytechnics are exempted from graduate level practicums or internships.

4. Building up School Networks

The Law coordinates educational institutions of all types and forms school networks throughout Macao. There are two types of school networks: the public school network and the private school network. The former covers government schools and private schools that receive governmental aid; the latter refers to private schools not in receipt of governmental aid. The Law requires that wherever possible the DSEJ should make sure that the distribution of schools corresponds to the distribution of population in different districts; accordingly, the DSEJ should allocate land for building schools where needed. Meanwhile, the Law seeks to ensure that there are enough schools in the public network by giving an appropriate level of governmental aid to private schools, and by indirectly supporting development in private schools outside the official network.

The establishment of the public school network has been a landmark of the provision of free education in Macao. The historic dominance of private schools in Macao has been a huge obstacle to the implementation of free education. Where the government cannot buy the rights to run a private school from the sponsoring bodies, it can still provide financial aid to schools. The public school network serves as a basis by which such financial assistance can be allocated. Many private schools do not have enough funding to run themselves efficiently. By receiving financial aid from the government, they can build and maintain more facilities and provide a more attractive package for their teaching staff. As a result, many private schools have been willing to join the public school network.

5. Defining Educational Institutions

This Law makes clear that educational institutions should be considered as serving public interests. Two types of school can be distinguished: publicly run and privately run educational institutions. Both types of institution enjoy academic autonomy. And by law, privately run educational institutions enjoy administrative and financial autonomy, while remaining subject to monitoring from the DSEJ. Privately run educational institutions can further be divided into two sub-categories: profit making and non-profit making. Not-for-profit schools generally adopt one of the following two practices: either they take no tuition fees or other charges, or they take tuition fees but plough them back into running the school. Either way, they are entitled to regular long-term subsidies from the DSEJ, subject to financial monitoring.

However, the Law does not state what the monitoring rights of the DSEJ are over privately run education institutions, profit making or non-profit making, or how the DSEJ should exercise such rights. This loophole has been the central ground of private schools' resistance to reform by the DSEJ.

6. Establishing the Language of Instruction

During the colonial era, for political reasons, classes were either taught in Portuguese or Chinese. In government-run schools, the primary language was Portuguese, with Chinese taught as a second language; in private schools, the opposite was the case. During the discussions leading up to the passing of the Law, the colonial government sought to tie the implementation of free education to the promotion of the Portuguese language. This was resisted strongly by the Chinese community, and the colonial government eventually backed down.

Consequently, non-profit making private schools generally taught in Chinese, with the second language being English. Similarly, the second language of English-oriented private schools was usually Chinese. Portuguese became an optional or promotional course and thus was not included in the formal curriculum. This was a big blow to the colonial government's plan to leave a cultural mark on Macao.

7. Establishing Funds for Education

This Law states that the funding of education is a shared responsibility of the DSEJ and the family of students. The Law requires that in formulating financial budget, the Macao SAR government should give priority to education. By law, the DSEJ should allocate funding to publicly run and privately run educational institutions according to the principles of equity and justice. In particular, the DSEJ should allocate regular funding to private schools and provide tuition-fee subsidies to private-school students. The Law requires that public funding allocated to private schools should be in the following three formats: first, regular subsidies to private schools for the general expenses on their daily operation; second, irregular subsidies to private schools for part of expenses on their infrastructure or for expenses on improving the learning environment for students and the professional training for teachers; and third, loans at a special rate.

8. Making a Clear Organization Chart for Management

This Law makes clear the division of labour and management within the Macao SAR government in coordinating educational institutions. The formulation of educational policies fell to the Governor (the highest administrator in Macao at the time); the implementation of educational policies fell to the education bureau (i.e., the DSEJ), which included oversight of planning, management, assessment, and the monitoring of the education system. Finally, the management of privately run educational institutions fell to their sponsoring bodies.

The Law makes it clear that the education system operates on the basis of ensuring the autonomy and freedom of sponsoring bodies, that different domains of the education system should be well coordinated, that the education system should ensure the democratic participation of every stakeholder in education, and that the education system should aim to achieve the dual goal of education and teaching standards. In regard to managing the education system, the Law also requires overall societal participation in education, so that there are appropriate platforms for teachers, students, families, and representatives of associations from social or education or cultural or economic domains. To this end, the colonial government at the time formed the educational committee. The committee sought to bring in different social forces to cooperate with each other to review the educational policies of the time and the overall education system, with a view to enhancing the further development of educational policies in Macao. The educational committee was influential at this time in formulating educational policies and the monitoring of executive departments in education.

In order to maximize the diversity of its composition, the educational committee recruited social leaders from different fields. However, in order to meet the special and unique needs of education, the committee set up a regular sub-committee formed solely of educators in Macao.

The Law also specifies how educational institutions should operate. It includes a requirement that there should be administrator-led and academic-led sections in each institution so as to facilitate a clear division of labour within the institution. In regard to school administration, the Law also insures the rights to participation of teachers, parents, and students, which is in line with the principle of democratic participation in education stated above.

9. Formulating Plans for Curriculum Development

There has been no standardized or common curriculum in Macao. Even a framework for a curriculum does not exist. The colonial government aimed to design a Macao-specific curriculum but it was strongly resisted at the time. In view of the fact that most Chinese students would complete their higher education outside of Macao (in mainland China, Taiwan, Hong Kong, and countries in the West), many private schools simply adopted the curriculum of those places. This practice was so long-standing that it gained the patina of "tradition", with many private schools unwilling to initiate change that would go against that tradition. This reinforced the general tendency of private schools to resist a common curriculum, lest their academic autonomy be restricted.

That being the case, the Law is multiply oriented when it comes to curriculum design. There are six broad parts to this section of the Law. First, the development of curriculum should take into account of the academic level of different educational stages and hence sets corresponding goals; in this way, the development of students in regard to their physical, intellectual, aesthetic, social, and moral aspects could be enhanced. Second, the design of curriculum should be only gradually reformed. Third, the direction of curriculum reform should be in line with principles that respect the academic autonomy of sponsoring bodies. Fourth, curriculum reform should tackle the issue of the language of instruction in balancing the use of Portuguese and Chinese. Fifth, one main focus of curriculum reforms should be on the cultivation of moral and civic consciousness of students. And sixth, curriculum reforms should ensure that the curriculum of senior secondary education is flexible enough to lead students to a variety of routes to progression – whether to the workplace or to further education.

Apart from reforming the formal curriculum, the Law also brings in the idea of a second curriculum – extra-curricular activities – in order to balance against the biases of the formal curriculum. Therefore students' potentials could be developed to the full, their cultural and civic knowledge bolstered, and their participation in sports activities and art education and social affairs enhanced.

Achievements

The law 11/91/M came into effect in 1991. Established in a hurry, a number of its deficiencies were only discovered in retrospect. Moreover, in that it only sought to provide a basic legal framework for education, it was not necessarily responsible for the delays and inefficiencies in applying its strictures. In the years before the 1999 handover of Macao to the PRC, a number of decrees were added as adjuncts to the basic framework, each seeking to concretize the general principles laid down in the Basic Law. These supplementary decrees generally focused on ten areas. (1) The constitutions of privately run educational establishments; (2) assistance to privately run educational establishments; (3) monitoring of privately run educational establishments; (4) free education; (5) curriculum development; (6) special education; (7) adult education; (8) vocational and technical education; (9) the career prospects of teachers; and (10) teacher training.

Despite its initial inadequacies and oversights, there is no dispute that the law 11/91/M is a landmark of the development of education in Macao. The passing of this law led to seventeen achievements before the 1999 handover.

First, the organizational structure of the DSEJ was finalized. Second, the constitutions for privately run educational institutions in the sector of basic education were set. Third, the operational format of accounting for non-profit-making educational institutions was passed and then monitored. Fourth, the activities of the association of parents and guardians were regulated. Fifth, the guiding frameworks for the curriculums of childhood education, pre-primary education, and primary education were designed. Sixth, the new system of students' welfare funds and social-cum-educational assistance were approved. Seventh, the developmental frameworks for the three domains of adult education – recurrent education, continuing education, and social education – were set. Eighth, regulations for teaching staff of educational institutions covered by the public school network were designed. Ninth, the system of special education was approved. Tenth, vocational and technical education was regulated. Eleventh, the criteria for the suspension of education were finalized. Twelfth, the legal foundation for academic supervisory activities conducted within schools was designed. Thirteenth, the legal system of teacher training at different educational stages was set. Fourteenth, a guiding framework for the curriculum of senior secondary education was designed. Fifteenth, the legal foundation for art education was approved. Sixteenth, it was affirmed that compulsory basic education will be provided for children and teenagers aged between 5 and 15. And seventeenth, the regulation for the hiring of teaching staff hired by public schools was approved.

THE LAW 9/2006

Macao was returned to the PRC on 20 December 1999. The Macao SAR government was then established. Yet education in Macao was still facing great challenges. While Law 11/91/M had laid the legal foundation for the development of education in Macao, Basic Law no.121 obliged the Macao SAR government to design its own educational policies, including the format of its education system and management, the language of instruction, how funding for education should be allocated, the format of its examination system, the form of the accreditation system for different qualifications, and how education in Macao should be promoted and developed. Indeed, Law 1/1999 no.3, Sections 1 and 5, state that except where the Basic Law is contradicted, previously existing laws, decrees and supplementary legal requirements should be adopted by the Macao SAR government. In other words, the Macao SAR government is required to make corresponding changes whenever contradictions arise. Given that Law 11/91/M was passed in a rush and that there were quite a number of loopholes, the number of revisions since should come as no surprise.

The Basic Law is essentially a constitutional document. This means that its contents are statements of principle – and therefore theoretical and abstract – rather than instructions for best practice. For example, according to the Basic Law, while the Macao SAR government should implement compulsory education, the sponsoring bodies of private schools are guaranteed complete autonomy. One result of this was that even after the 1999 handover, private schools continued to recruit staff from outside Macao and teach the curriculum from other countries. While the Basic Law was set up to respect the colonial history of Macao and the particular divisions this wrought, it has not had the effect of changing the system. Constitutionally, the Macao education system remains privately run yet publicly funded. Indeed, the Basic Law could be seen to guarantee this system in perpetuity.

Underlying Concerns

While the initial transition of the education law was smooth, the public gradually saw and felt the need to review the existing education system. In 2002, the Macao SAR government started the daunting task of revising the education law of Macao; extending consultations into the public and professional spheres. Indeed in June 2003, two proposals on reforming the Macao education system were drafted for public and professional consultations. There were four major concerns. The first was about extending coverage from ten years of free basic education to twelve. Where should the coverage be extended: to pre-school education or senior secondary education? The second issue was the proposal to turn the education model into a 6-3-3 system: with six years of primary education, three years of junior secondary education, and three years of senior education. Would such a standardized system jeopardise Macao's reputation for educational diversity? The third issue was about how to use educational funds more effectively. And the fourth was about the careers of teachers hired by private schools – a perennial problem focusing on the tendency for such teachers to be both overloaded with work and underpaid.

The process of consultation lasted for three whole years. Finally, the law 9/2006 was passed on 13 December 2006. It addresses twelve specific concerns. Let us turn to them one by one.

1. Defining the Non-Tertiary Education System

While the law 11/91/M is about the entire Macao education system, the law 9/2006 clearly states that it is only about the Macao non-tertiary education system, leaving the sector of higher education for another law. Non-tertiary education is constituted of the formal education system and the continuing education system. The former includes childhood education, primary education, secondary education (junior and secondary levels), vocational and technical education, and special education; and the latter refers to family education, recurrent education, community education, vocational training, and other educational activities.

2. Confirming the Principals Underlying the Education System

This Law seeks to ensure the right of everyone to education. Public or individual entities (e.g., teachers) are meant to create an environment conducive to education, to ensure the flexibility and diversity of that education, and to make sure that different ethnic or social communities can integrate and live in harmony. The Macao SAR government provides each learner with an equal opportunity for assessing the education on offer to them and thereby to achieve educational success. It furthermore stressed that continuing education could be developed sustainably based on the principle of life-long learning, so that the competitiveness of Macao can be maintained and enhanced. Under this part of the law, the Macao SAR government respects the freedom to teach and to learn, and does its best to defend such freedom, in the hope of developing talents of various kinds for a challenging and uncertain future.

3. Setting the Overall Goals of Education

This Law makes clear that Macao should strive to nurture learners to love the country and the region of Macao, to be compassionate, to obey rules and laws, to cultivate a sense of responsibility in learners, to enable learners to exercise their rights and yet take up their duties, and to develop learners' democratic and civic virtues, so that they can get along with each other and care about social issues. Through education, learners should be acculturated by the Chinese culture but learn to respect the unique characteristics of Macao, and therefore respect the coexistence of multi-cultures and thus develop a tolerant worldview. Through education, learners should also be equipped with the knowledge of sciences and humanity, and therefore become creative and uphold a sustainable development worldview and materialize the principle of life-long learning. And through education, the ability of learners to appreciate aesthetics should be enhanced, thereby bringing people into closer contact with nature.

4. Designing the Compulsory Education System and the Free Education System

This Law makes clear that it is compulsory for children or teenagers aged between 5 and 15 to receive a basic education. Apart from the Macao SAR government and educational institutions, parents are also responsible for making sure that those mentioned above should receive a basic education. Beneficiaries of free education refer to those Macao residents studying in public schools or private schools that join the school network. Beneficiaries are exempt from paying the tuition fees, supplementary fees, and other fees related to registration, studies, and certificates. This Law requires that 15-year free education should be implemented state-wide before the school year of 2009/2010.

5. Setting the Principals Underlying Curriculum and Pedagogy

This Law requires that the design of curriculum should be aligned with the basic principles underlying the education system and the overall educational goals stated above, as well as the educational goals specific to each educational stage and/or each form of education. The Macao SAR government should set the framework of the curriculum at different educational stages and the basic academic requirements at each educational stage. Under this requirement, public schools or private schools can design their own school-specific curriculums. This Law requires that the contents of childhood education should be mostly integrated knowledge; at the primary or junior secondary level the focus should be on the integration and interdependence between subjects; at the senior secondary level the curriculum should take into account the requirements of higher education and employment. Meanwhile, vocational and technical education should include internships and practicums in response to the market needs as well as the needs of higher education. Special education should focus on individualized learning.

Apart from the formal curriculum, this Law also states that the second curriculum or extra-curricular activities – mostly about sports or art or community activities – should enhance the all-round development of students. This Law also makes clear that there should be multiple means of assessment in order to enable students to succeed.

6. Identifying Assistance to Students

This Law ensures a provision system of educational assistance to students, in order to ensure that every student has an equal opportunity for education and to improve their all-round development. Educational assistance refers to a variety of supporting measures, such as school counselling and advice on educational and career development. Educational assistance is provided to students who are still receiving a compulsory education and is meant to ensure that they are provided with an equal opportunity for education and to do well academically. Educational assistance includes insurance fees for students and subsidies for students whose families have financial difficulties. It includes tuition fees allowances, meal allowances, learning aids allowances, facilities for learning allowances, and also free health protection.

7. Defining Educational Institutions and the Schooling System

According to this Law, there are two types of educational institutions: publicly run and privately run. The former are run by the Macao SAR government and the latter by sponsoring bodies. Sponsoring bodies can enjoy tax exemptions or tax deductions. This Law states that publicly run educational institutions enjoy academic autonomy, in addition to administrative and financial autonomy.

The schooling system is constituted of public schools and private schools. The system of free education consists of the formal education provided by public schools and the free education provided by private schools. Only non-profit-making local private schools could join the system of free education. The entire schooling system is taken care of by the Macao SAR government.

8. Setting the Language of Instruction and the School Management System

This Law requires that public schools should adopt one of the two official languages (Portuguese or Chinese) as the language of instruction. Private schools could choose the official languages, or other languages, as their primary language of instruction. Private schools choosing other languages need to submit documents to the Macao SAR government for approval. In addition, they should also provide students with an opportunity for learning at least one official language.

This Law seeks to facilitate the participation of the teaching staff, students, parents, and other educators in education. Sponsoring bodies should set up a school board, appoint board members, and design its constitution stating the rights and duties of board members and the formation and operation of school board. The constitutions of school boards set by private schools should be subject to the approval of the Macao SAR government. The school board should appoint a principal to take care of the daily operation of the school; and, each school should set up departments of administration, counselling, and teaching and learning.

9. Securing Human Resources for Education

This Law states that teaching staff and members of educational institutions should comply with their school's respective requirements for teaching a specific subject or field at a given educational stage in a particular education system. The promotion of a teaching staff member should take into account three factors: seniority, professional development, and performance. There are distinct legal frameworks for establishing duties and rights, the work type, rank, appraisal, workload, salaries and benefits, and retirement benefits for teaching staff working in public and private schools. This Law insures the rights and duties of teaching staff to professional development. Through training, self-learning, research, and practical help, the DSEJ should provide teaching staff with resources and opportunities for professional development.

10. Securing Material Resources for Schools

This Law states that in planning the urban development of Macao, the SAR government should take the need for the development of education into consideration, sparing land for schools and related facilities as required. In addition, the SAR government should consider seriously the practicability and effectiveness of proposals sent by private schools and their relevance to general educational policies, and then provide corresponding aid and support. This Law ensures that students should have a good learning environment, by setting specific requirements on school buildings, school space for a variety of activities, school facilities, and the maximum number of students that a school should take. This Law states that the SAR government should encourage schools and communities to be open to each other and develop closely together. This Law requires that schools should comply with the guidance set by the DSEJ in assigning spaces for storing teaching material and teaching aids, storing information, setting up library and laboratories and craftwork studios, and building rooms and storing facilities for sports and art.

11. Making Clear Funding for Education

This Law states clearly that educational expenses should be jointly borne by the Macao SAR government and families. In designing a financial budget, the SAR government should give priority to expenses for non-tertiary education. The Macao SAR government should provide educational aid based on the principles of equity and justice. Beneficiaries should use the aids effectively, with the government maintaining the right to monitor how the aids are used.

The Macao SAR government should provide free education subsidies to non-profit-making private schools that join the school network so that they can pay the cost of daily operation and general expenses. The SAR government should invest resources in recurrent education to encourage the life-long learning of Macao residents. The SAR government should also provide tuition fees subsidies to students who enroll in private schools but do not benefit from the free education system. The SAR government should provide allowances for professional development to the teaching staff in private schools. Apart from these assertions, this Law states that the fund for educational development should support the development of non-tertiary education, including educational plans and activities such as (1) plans for school improvement, (2) improving the schooling environment and facilities, (3) improving school-based curriculum and pedagogy, (4) enhancing professional development of teachers, (5) insuring a balanced development of students, (6) aiding the development of special education, and (7) promoting the further development of continuing education.

12. Implementing the Education System and Its Assessment

This Law requires that the Macao SAR government should formulate educational policies. Through consulting educational committees formed by different civil associations, the Macao SAR government can enhance social participation in the development of education. The DSEJ should be responsible for implementing educational policies and monitoring such implementations. The SAR government is responsible for promoting and aiding research activities in the field of education. With a view to improving the quality of education, the educational committee should follow up on the development of a system of assessments and its implementation, in the hope that the development of education can keep pace with the needs arising from the development of Macao and the global development.

Law 9/2006 about non-tertiary education was passed at the same time as Law 19/2006 (about the regulation of free education subsidies) and Law 20/2006 (about the system of tuition fees subsidies). The latter two specify concretely the actual financial limits of various kinds of subsidies. For example, free education subsidies to each private school are based on the number of classes with a quorum (minimum amount) of students; any further subsidy is based on a formula derived from this quorum. In addition, Law 19/2006 requires that private schools should not expel students on unreasonable grounds and should not refuse to take students when the number of students is less than a set quota.

CONCLUDING REMARKS

For the majority of the period of Portuguese colonial rule, education for the local Chinese population was substantially – if not completely – neglected. With the date for the handover of Macao from Portuguese to Chinese rule looming, the colonial government finally set up a basic education law covering all residents of Macao: Law 11/91M. Despite the inadequacies of the law, and the rush in which it was drafted, Law 11/91/M can still be seen as a landmark in the development of education in Macao. The law was revised through sub-decrees before the handover and then strengthened thereafter. Law 9/2006 is itself imperfect, but has laid the foundation of educational practice in every institution in modern Macao. This, therefore, is the general legal background in which we shall discuss the case of private schools in Macao today.

Chapter 6

SCHOOLS

In this chapter, we shall examine the practices of schools in running their business, so to speak, and in regulating students and teachers. We argue that despite receiving increasing levels of government subsidies since 1999, private schools remain unaccountable to the public. We further argue that the practices of control and regulation over both teachers and staff do not support the overall professionalism of their teaching staff or the provision of quality education. In fact, these practices have one main aim, which is to ensure the survival of the school itself by full enrolment. In order to exert control over students, the school management invariably keeps a tight hold on its teachers.

We shall first recapitulate the historical background against which the general practices of private schools have developed. We shall then discuss the relationship between the ethos of a particular sponsoring body and the type of schools it runs. Using interviews with students and teachers, drawn from a number of research projects we conducted, we shall seek to illustrate how private schools regulate their students and teaching staff. The chapter will conclude with a discussion of the unaccountability of private schools to the government and the public, and the concomitant effects this can have on both the quality of education on offer and the professionalism of the teachers who offer it.

BRIEF HISTORICAL BACKGROUND

Because Macao's colonial school system dealt only with the children of Portuguese settlers, the task of educating the local Chinese population fell to voluntary and civic organizations. As a result, most schools in Macao are private schools. These private schools have been run by individuals, religious organizations, trading organizations, neighbourhood associations, lineage associations, and the Federation of Labour Union (Clayton, 2009). As discussed in Chapter 4, the '12.3 Incident' of 1966 saw the withdrawal of pro-KMT schools from Macao. The gap was filled by so-called "traditional organizations", who were almost invariably pro-PRC.

Since 1966, three major types of school can be identified: government schools, Catholic schools, and schools run by traditional organizations. With some fluctuations, Catholic schools and schools run by traditional organizations have dominated education for the Chinese population in Macao – with some help from private schools run by other Christian denominations and by non-traditional organizations. (We denote these as 'Other Schools' in the Tables below.)

In the school year of 2011-2012, there were 78 licensed schools in Macao (the license pertaining to all stages of basic education). 11 of these schools were government administered, while 67 were privately run. In other words just 14% of all schools in Macao are public schools. Table 6.1 lists the distribution of primary and secondary schools by school type in Macao in that school year.

Table 6.1. Distribution of schools by schooling organization in Macao in the school year of 2011-2012

School type	Number of primary schools	Number of secondary schools	Total number of schools	Proportion
Government schools	5	3	8	7.5%
Catholic schools	23	16	39	36.4%
Schools run by traditional organizations	23	15	38	35.5%
Other schools	13	9	22	20.6%
Total	64	43	107	100.0%

Table 6.1 shows that despite an overall showing of 14% for the government sector, only about 7.5% of primary and secondary schools are government schools. Roughly one-third are Catholic schools, while a third are run by traditional organizations. About one-fifth are categorized as 'Other'.

This pattern of distribution has been more or less consistent since the 1980s (see Tables 6.2 and 6.3). In the school year of 1983-1984 and that of

1988-1989, about 13-15% of schools were government schools and about 30-40% were Catholic schools. At the same time, the number of schools organized by individuals and public enterprises seemed to decline (they were often taken over by traditional organizations), while the proportion of schools run by traditional organizations has fluctuated: it was about 50% in the school year of 1983-1984, decreasing to about 20% in the school year of 1988-1989, before increasing to over 30% in the school year of 2011-2012. Nevertheless, the general composition of school management in Macao has remained by and large stable.

Table 6.2. Distribution of schools by schooling organization in Macao in the school year of 1983-1984

Schooling organization	Number of schools	Proportion of schools
The Portuguese colonial government	23	13.1%
The Catholic Church	48	27.3%
Non-profit making organizations	90	51.1%
Co-operation organizations	2	1.1%
Public enterprises	1	0.6%
Others	12	6.8%
Total	176	100.0%

Source: A report conducted by the Portuguese colonial government collected by the second author.

Since the 1999 handover, the Macao SAR government has invested more resources in basic education; in addition, it has made effort to improve education law. It finally replaced the old Fundamental Law of Non-tertiary Education (Law 11/91/M) with a new one (the law 9/2006) in 2006. The education model stabilized into a 6+3+3 composition under this new law, but the following issues remain problematic, or at least debatable. First, despite providing more resources of all kinds to private schools, the Macao SAR government is rather ineffective in monitoring how private schools spend the subsidies or resources they receive. This is because private schools are fundamentally accountable to their sponsoring organizations, rather than the government or the public. The 2006 law further guaranteed the academic autonomy of Macao's private schools, which means that there is huge variance in the curriculums and management standards private schools employ. For instance, private schools can set their own criteria for student admissions, and even where a school may run the same curriculum as another private school, they will have varying means of assessing both teachers and students. This variability extends to how schools regulate the conduct of their students, and the rules governing how students can be disqualified or expelled. A similar picture prevails in regard to teachers, who are hired to school-specific requirements, and are monitored, disciplined and sometimes removed from post by similarly unique standards. Teachers and students are therefore both part of a system that does not consistently address either their needs or their failings. Let us look first at the students.

Table 6.3. Distribution of school types in Macao in the school year of 1988-89

School type	Number of schools	Proportion of schools
Public schools	12	14.8%[--------]
Private schools	69	85.2%[100%]
Religious		47.7%[56%]
Catholic		40.0%[47%]
Protestant		7.7%[09%]
Civil society		37.5%[44%]
Traditional organizations		20.5%[24%]
Individuals		17.0%[20%]
Total	81	100.0%[------]

Source: Wong, 1991, p.39 Tables 1 and 2.

Regulation of Students

Each private school in Macao has its own educational mission and seeks to nurture students of a particular type. However, private schools receive government resource and funding broadly in line with the number of students they can attract, which has the effect of making students, first and foremost, a source of revenue. This situation has become more complicated since the passing of the Basic Law. Under the Portuguese colonial government, private schools received no direct subsidy from government. While small amounts of funding were made available in the run up to the 1999 handover to the PRC – and while the amounts have steadily increased since – the majority of funds an average private school receives will be based on student enrollment.

As shown in Chapter 2, SAR government funds are not provided for each student as an individual but for each class of a particular grade. In order to get to a particular subsidy level, every school has to make sure that the class size reaches a particular number of students. To attract students and persuade their parents, private schools have to build up their reputation. They generally seek to construct an image of themselves as academically outstanding and socially useful. However, in the absence of standardized examinations, there are no readily agreed indicators of how academically outstanding a particular school is. This is partly why private schools seek to highlight discipline and rigor in their classrooms. This emphasis on student conduct is not false in practice (as will be seen), but it is at least partly fictive: it aims to convince parents that a well-behaved student is one who will succeed academically.

As mentioned before, private schools do have their own strong moral, social and ethical codes – usually drawn from the sponsoring organization – but these genuine concerns often go hand in hand with an unimaginative concentration on rules for rules' sake. In this part of the chapter, we shall concentrate on how private schools manage their students through three headings: admission, regulation and disqualification. We shall argue that the practices private schools employ in these areas are not intended to provide for a student's individual needs or to meet a certain standard of education in general; rather, the practices are intended to bolster the schools' reputations and thereby secure their financial survival.

Admission

Private schools have always competed for students in Macao. While schools generally start their recruitment of students in similar style – circulating application forms and stating the general recruitment criteria – there is simply no standardization across the private school sector. Parents therefore have to familiarize themselves with the practices of each apparently suitable school. And this process begins right at the start of a child's education: putting the name of a child down for a particular kindergarten generally implies that the child will be a sent to a primary school run by the same organisation, and then onto a secondary school run by the same organisation. Even where that is not possible, there are generally local agreements and affiliations between schools at each stage, whereby the three sectors of education (pre-school, primary, and secondary) are generally tied together in an informal process of recruitment. We might describe this as a 'through-train' model of education. Parents are therefore keen to make the right choice at pre-school level, because which kindergarten a child attends very often dictates the next twelve years of their academic life.

This situation has not greatly changed since the 1999 handover. There is little government effort in, for instance, centralising the allocation of students to different kindergartens. This means that parents generally apply for several at once. (The application and interview period for well-known kindergartens tend to be quite early in the year; the deadline for the less well-known kindergartens is usually much later.) Parents must therefore prepare their children for several different types of admission processes. At first glance, pre-primary schools are free and accessible to all. And while it is true that tuition fees are provided by the government, kindergartens often charge lunch fees, air-conditioning fees, snack fees, fees for extra classes, etc. A well connected kindergarten – operating as a feeder channel for a well-regarded primary school – will often have very high fees of this sort. Hence, while there is no official league table of schools at any level in Macao, there is an unofficial ranking based on parents' perceptions both of what they want and what they think they will get. Adding to this is the opaque nature of the admission criteria. The first author of this book has had two conversations with teachers who point out that having been a past pupil oneself is often a boon to the selection of one's own children, as are social connections with staff and board members. From these conversations:

> 'I remember, there was a long queue outside that kindergarten – parents were so keen to send their children to that well-known kindergarten. (…) I heard that the application fee was over 100,000MOP. (…) In the end, if you know the principal, your child would be granted an interview.' (A teacher, personal communication with the first author)

> 'Secondary school X is the best school in Macao; every parent wants to get their children into its kindergarten. (…) You know how expensive it is to study there! (…) Yet parents' wealth is not the whole story; what also matters is parents' social networks. (…) In the past, children of its alumni had a good shot. (…) But now it isn't true anymore. (…) I heard that parents have to get a recommendation letter from its board members before they could send in their applications. (A teacher, personal communication with the first author)

Without centralization, parents have to apply individually to each school so as to get their children into a school of their choice. Without standardization, each school arranges their own means of recruitment, and set up their own recruitment criteria. Despite receiving public subsidies, private schools are not accountable to the public and therefore not obliged to make this process of recruitment transparent to the public. As a result, people often complain that nepotism matters in Macao and that what counts in getting a child into a well-known school is his/her parents' social connections. Perhaps unsurprisingly as a result, class segregation of schools is observed in Macao. Although a systematic investigation has not been conducted, the first author's observations on recruiting students from three secondary schools are relevant. From the top-ranked school, only one of nineteen students could be said to have come from a disadvantaged background (her father being a manual worker; the other eighteen have parents who are professionals, managers, administrators, even employers. Of the lowest-ranking school, eight of the sixteen students had parents who were running a small business, and none of the parents belonged to the professional class.

Regulation

In order to build up their reputation and compete for students, private schools usually focus on promoting a school's academic standing and overall values. This effectively makes the performance and conduct of existing students a key persuading factor. This, in turn, explains the style of student regulation often practiced in private schools in Macao.

As explained in Chapter 2, in the absence of a common curriculum for Macao, private schools are free to teach a curriculum of their own. Generally, this means adopting a Taiwanese curriculum, a Hong Kong curriculum, a PRC curriculum, or some mixture of the above. This is especially true where private secondary schools have formal links with universities in mainland China or Taiwan, whereby top-performing students often receive conditional offers from universities before they have graduated from secondary school. In a sense, this means that education in Macao is always focused on progression to the next stage (or next institution), rather than on the particular stage of education a student is actually at. The freestyle approach to curriculum design is mirrored (and to some extent complicated) by a similar approach to examinations. Private schools effectively design their own, meaning there is no means of assessing one student against another across Macao. Schools often place great emphasis on the regularity of their testing, and on the fact that they hold students back a year if they are not felt to be performing academically (Wong, 2013). In fact, grade retention might be said to be a deliberate policy in some schools in Macao. The overall accumulative rate of grade retention in Macao is among the highest in OECD countries, or in regions participating in PISA. Table 6.4 summarizes the major criteria for retention in private schools in Macao.

Table 6.4. Examples of criteria for in-grade retention used by 43 secondary schools

Criterion for grade retention	Remarks
Conduct	Poor conduct (e.g., below grade B or C) could lead to in-grade retention in 10 schools.
Academic performance 1. Passing marks	Schools set different passing marks, ranging from 40 to 60 out of 100 marks.
2. Weighting	All except 8 schools differentiate core subjects from the others or give more weighting to core subjects (e.g., core subjects are usually weighed with a greater number of units). Chinese, English, Mathematics are usually three core subjects or subjects with double weightings.
Specific concern 1. The maximum number of units/subjects students could fail without being retained	This number ranges from one unit of a core subject to six peripheral subjects. 7 schools require students to repeat a grade if they fail the same subject in two consecutive years.
2. Maximum number of retention allowed	Only 7 schools set a maximum number of retentions each grade. 6 schools allow students to get retained only once. If asked to repeat a further year, students are either asked or obliged to quit the school.

It is indisputable that private schools want to uphold a decent academic standard. However, the truth is that no private schools have explained what academic standards they seek to uphold. Making things worse is the general format of evaluation: most questions in quizzes, tests, and examinations are "what" questions or fact-recognition questions that rely on students memorising facts. The following quotations are very good examples:

'My colleagues usually ask students questions about fact-recognition. (…) And I was new to the school and wanted to make a suggestion to the upcoming test. (…) So, I suggested that perhaps out of 100 marks, we could spare 20 marks on some open-ended questions to see students' analytical ability. (…) My colleagues turned it down; they said that it would create problems in marking – how to grade those open-ended questions? They don't want confusion and want that there is only one correct answer to each question. (…) Then, what could I do? They just didn't listen to me and said that I was too inexperienced in designing tests.' (A teacher, personal communication with the first author)

'I was teaching Geography in the 1970s. (…) I was teaching a class of students a Hong Kong curriculum and a Taiwan curriculum at the same time and preparing them for public examinations held in these two places. When going through those past examination papers, I realised that expectations of students differed in these two places. (…) Many questions in Taiwan are about facts. For example, students are asked about the height of a particular mountain. (…) By contrast, in the Hong Kong Curriculum, students are expected to understand the basic facts and apply them in responding to a question. (…) For example, students are given a map with different symbols; so students have to understand the meanings of those symbols. Then, students are asked questions like "If you are going to build a wood factory, where would you like to set it up? Why?". (…) It's clear that memorising basic facts won't give students a high score. Students have to give the reasoning behind their choice. (…) I think, the format of evaluation matters in influencing how students learn. (…) The format in Hong Kong is more conducive to cultivating students' logical reasoning and analytical ability, which are essential to an independent thinker.' (A retired teacher, in an interview from a series of in-depth interviews by the authors)

Simply put, there are many assessments, of different weightings, conducted in each private school throughout an academic year, and there are a variety of passing marks set by different private schools. In many schools, there are weekly dictations, weekly quizzes, monthly tests, and end-of-semester examinations; and the passing marks range from 40 to 60. Yet the format of assessment is broadly the same: students are expected to memorize facts by rote. Their scores are then used as an indicator of the academic standard of their school. Some private schools also place emphasis on their rates of grade retention – how many students fail to get promoted to the following grade – and refer to such rates as an indicator that their schools are academically demanding. A teacher makes this point clearly:

> 'Most schools are private schools here and their survival depends on student enrolment. Then, how could schools attract students, actually their parents? No one wants to admit it, but it's an open secret that many school principals use grade retention as a device to get rid of so-called poor students. ... Some years ago, when a principal increased the retention rate drastically, he retained a great number of students who would've been promoted in many other schools. The principal was severely criticized for sacrificing students' futures for the sake of building up the school reputation. In just a few years' time, this school has become one of the top schools in Macao that many parents desperately want to send their children to. So now, who else remembers those severe criticisms? (...) Many schools actually follow suit in the hope that they could boost up their school reputations.' (A teacher, in a focus group interview conducted by the first author)

It is doubtful that such practices of private schools are meant to uphold a decent academic standard if we accept that learning is not merely about fact recognition. Rather, we argue that frequent testing is usually a means of giving the impression of academic rigor. Likewise, retaining students is mostly designed to give the impression that the school is academically demanding and tough on failure.

Leaving aside purely academic issues, private schools take great pains to regulate the conduct of students. As most private schools represent a particular ethos or trade, they will tend to nurture students in the image of that ethos or trade. But the day-to-day monitoring of this process is carried out in the playground or the classroom, with no real focus on cultivating specific desirable qualities for the future. Thus, while schools may have different overall goals, the main emphasis in all private schools is to ensure that their students are quiet and obedient. Table 6.5 provides some examples of school regulations from each of the four types of school in Macao.

Put simply, private schools in Macao basically demand students' absolute obedience. The following example perhaps seems rather extreme but they are telling about the broader culture of education in Macao. A well-known secondary school sets up the following two school regulations: students have to obey teachers and seniors at all times in all places; students are not allowed to challenge the above school regulation. Indeed, it is not uncommon to hear students in Macao complain about how unreasonably their teachers treat them.

Table 6.5. Examples of school regulations from four types of schools in Macao

School type	School regulations about students' behaviour in classroom
Government schools	- Respect and obey teachers - Be attentive and obey classroom rules in classes and submit assignments on time - Keep the same seat after being assigned by the form teacher
Schools organized by traditional organizations	- Be quiet in classes, respect teachers, work hard - Get into classroom immediately after the recess and wait quietly for the next class - Queue up quickly, quietly, and in an orderly fashion to leave the school
Schools organized by the Catholic Church	- Respect and obey Sisters and teaching staff - No sleeping or talking in classes - Be attentive, polite, self-disciplined, and cooperative in classes
Other schools	- Be cooperative in classes - Should not read other books or assignments in classes - Should not disturb the class

'I'm so scared of teachers. (…) You just don't know when they'd give you a hard time. (…) I remember an instance: a student was warned by a teacher that his hair was too long and should have it cut; otherwise the student would get a demerit. (…) The following day, that student had all his hair cut – a skin-head like style. But he still got a demerit. The teacher said that although he didn't violate the school regulation concerning hair length, his action itself was a challenge to the teacher's authority. (…) So, you see, teachers are the law – they decide what should be punished even if there is no such regulation in black and white.' (A middle-ranking day-school student, in an individual interview conducted by the first author)

> 'A classmate of mine told me that she was found bringing her cell phone to school; but she was found after school on the street, by a teacher who was not teaching her. (…) I don't understand why teachers have power to enforce school regulations even after school. (…) We are all so scared of teachers.' (A student, in a focus group interview conducted by the first author)

> 'When I was in secondary school, we had to keep silence all the time. (…) We were not allowed to make any sound, even asking your neighbour quietly about what was going on in class. (…) You see, there is always absolute silence in most classrooms in Macao.' (A student doing a course of the first author, in class discussion)

In other words, students are required to yield to teachers' authority and teachers' authority is unchallengeable at all times. Students failing to comply with teachers' commands will be punished. As is shown in Table 6.4 above, students are even required to repeat a grade because of their conduct, which is usually judged by just a single teacher: their form teacher. It is questionable why conduct should be a criterion for grade retention, and such practices imply that grade retention is meant more to punish the disobedient than to help academically less capable students.

Disqualification

Disqualification is the most serious punishment for students who fail to meet schools' requirements in academic performance and conduct. As Table 6.4 above shows, in some schools students who fail to progress in two academic years (whether consecutive or not) are obliged to leave the school. The disciplinary reasons a student may be dismissed are straightforward enough: a violent assault on a classmate or teacher, for instance. More deserving of our attention are the students who are disqualified for academic reasons.

In the absence of a clear Macao-wide academic standard, this is very difficult to judge. And how is disqualification for academic under-achievement supposed to help students in the first place? Because schools compete with each other for students, a student who has been ejected from a certain school is effectively blacklisted from similar schools – because why would they take the cast-offs of their competitors? So disqualified students tend to end up at poorer ranked schools than the ones they have been ejected from. This process indirectly helps to keep low-ranked schools alive.

> 'I don't think grade retention works. What I have observed is that students who get retained do even worse in the following year – they lose the confidence and motivation. (...) Retention can't help students improve their academic performance. (...) I think grade retention is still practised perhaps because it could contribute to the survival of low-ranking schools by facilitating the physical mobility of students. Retained students kicked out of high-ranking schools are an important source of enrolment to low ranking schools. (...) You know, many schools ask students to quit school when they are retained for the second time. Without grade retention, many students would not have got kicked out of school and they would not have had to look for a place in a low ranking school.' (A teacher, personal communication with the first author)

In summary, we argue that the monitoring of private schools over students, in terms of academic performances and conduct, is not derived from any educational philosophy or out of concern for individual students' needs. Such practices are meant to enable schools to exert control over their students more effectively, so as to build up a reputation for the schools. In order to make sure that this control is exerted effectively and will succeed in making students obedient, submissive, and compliant, private schools have to rely on their teaching staff. This brings us to how private schools in Macao regulate their teaching staff.

REGULATION OF TEACHERS

It is indisputable good practice – for teachers and schools alike – that schools should hire staff according to recognisable qualifications, that they should set up some sort of monitoring programme for teachers, and that they should have measures in place that effect the removal of underperforming teachers from their jobs. In this section we look at how private schools hire, monitor and dispose of their teaching staff, arguing that such measures do not enhance teachers' professionalism, but actually contribute to their alienation.

Hiring

While public schools make up only a small fraction of schools in Macao, they receive an abundance of resources from the government, and teachers are offered an attractive and rewarding package to teach classes that are rarely bigger than 20 students. Teachers are hired to public schools by transparent and open recruitment. By contrast, private schools do not receive direct funding from government, and have been allowed to retain distinctive – not to say unique – management styles in which teachers are only accountable to the school's sponsoring body. This flexibility of management style extends to the grounds by which teachers are hired in the first place. Because most private schools operate on a tight budget, budgetary restrictions also apply to hiring.

Macao also had a generally low level of education well into the 1980s, and teacher training was also limited. For example, only 106 students graduated from the teacher training course at the University of Macau in 1988/89 (Wong, 1991:45).

The result has been that it has been difficult for private schools to be selective in teacher recruitment. It is therefore not surprising to see that most teachers recruited during the colonial period did not have a higher degree or a teaching diploma.

A study reported in Wong (1991) could be used as an additional example. As shown in Table 6.6, even in the late 1980s, only 54% of teachers were qualified to take up a teaching post; a significant minority – 46% – were not qualified at all. 34% had only a secondary qualification, 9% did not complete a teaching diploma (primary education), and 3% did not complete a bachelor's degree.

Given the small supply of qualified teachers in Macao, a teaching qualification obtained outside of Macao was also recognized. This remains the case to some extent today. As many teachers indicated (through personal communication with the first author), people with a degree from Hong Kong, Taiwan, the mainland China, or overseas would all be recognized in Macao.

In fact, people originating from Hong Kong, Taiwan, mainland China, or certain other non-Chinese societies would in principal have no difficulties in getting a teaching job in Macao as long as they have a higher qualification or a teaching diploma. In short, while there is a gap in qualification between teachers hired by public schools and those hired by private schools, there is in particular a huge variation in teachers' qualification across private schools.

Table 6.6. Qualifications of teachers in the school year 1987/1988

Teaching level	Secondary qualification	Teaching diploma (primary education)	Incomplete teaching diploma (primary education)	Bachelor's degree	Incomplete bachelor's degree	Total
Pre-primary	123	275	39	9	---	446
Primary	563	301	177	88	---	1129
Secondary	133	1	---	626	75	835
Total	819 (34%)	577 (24%)	216 (9%)	723 (30%)	75 (3%)	2410 (100%)

Source: Wong, 1991: p.42 Table 7.

In addition, the recruitment process also varies across schools. While there are set procedures in public schools, private schools can set up their own procedures without oversight by the Macao SAR government. Indeed, many teachers, either through personal communication with the first author or in focus group interviews conducted by the first author, indicated that what mattered in successful recruitment was not the qualification or attributes or personal qualities of prospective teachers but the personal inclination of principals.

> 'Macao is rather unusual. In many schools, the principal could decide whom to hire without being challenged. (...) It is not unheard of principals hiring teachers who do not necessarily match the positions required. (...) For example, a colleague of mine was doing Fashion Design at university but was hired to teach Geography; and I majored in the Chinese language but was asked to teach World History. (...) I heard from a friend that a colleague of his actually majored in Business Studies at university but was hired to teach the English language. (...) So, basically, it is a matter of the principal's liking – if the principal wants to hire that person, it doesn't really matter whether the person could teach the subject of his/her expertise.' (A teacher, personal communication with the first author)

> 'In many schools in Macao, the principal has the absolute power. (...) The procedures of recruitment vary; but it is never a transparent recruitment process. (...) And no one would question it. (...) The principal is the only one who has the say over whom to recruit. (...) No one dare to challenge the principal.' (A teacher, in a focus group interview conducted by the first author)

We shall return to the power of principals below. What is clear here is that given a small supply of qualified teachers in Macao, anyone who had some secondary qualification could get a teaching job. Given that private schools could have their own distinctive management style, the recruitment process was not transparent, leading to questions of the overall professionalism of teaching in Macao. Given such a variation in teachers' qualifications, it is also very likely that wages vary hugely across private schools.

Before government subsidies were first made available to private schools in 1977, it made a certain amount of sense that teachers' pay was low. In fact, in the 1950s and 60s, it was generally lower than that of a manual worker. The experience of a teacher respondent interviewed by the second author could be referred to for illustration. His experience was perhaps considered extreme. But it is telling about the financial situation of teachers in the colonial era and their social status at the time. In the 1970s, this man and his wife were both teachers but they found it rather hard to bring up two little children with their meagre wages. So, the couple decided that the wife should keep the teaching job while the husband should become a meter reader because of the much higher pay. Yet, because of his passion for teaching, he insisted on teaching part-time in an evening school. According to this teacher respondent, his experience was not an isolated incidence but rather common in that period in Macao. Private schools in this era in Macao were accountable to the sponsoring bodies that funded them. They were not obliged to be transparent about how they paid their teaching staff or how much work they assigned to them. Principals having absolute power on a day-to-day level, they also had sole oversight on the pay and workload of each teacher of the school. It was not until 2012 that teachers were guaranteed minimum pay or a maximum workload.

Unsurprisingly, even though a small amount of government money was extended to private schools from 1977, teachers in Macao essentially had extremely low pay, especially in comparison to the pay of public school teachers. The situation is reflected in a survey of 424 teachers conducted in the school year 1987/1988.

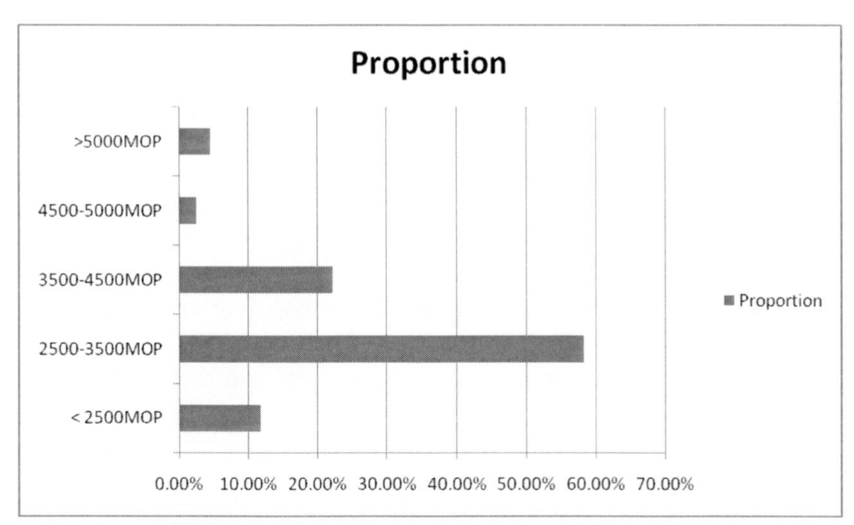

Source: Wong, 1991: p.184 Table 3.

Figure 6.1. The distribution of teachers in Macao by their pay (in MOP).

As summarised in Figure 6.1, teachers in private schools earned around 2,500 to 3,500MOP a month, which was much less than their public school counterparts who earned about 8,000 to 10,000MOP a month and got paid for 14 months a year.

Given the low pay, it is unsurprising that 25.7% of teachers in this study took up a part-time job in addition to their teaching job, as revealed in the same study. Figure 6.2 indicates that 60% of these teachers cited low pay as a reason for taking on extra work:

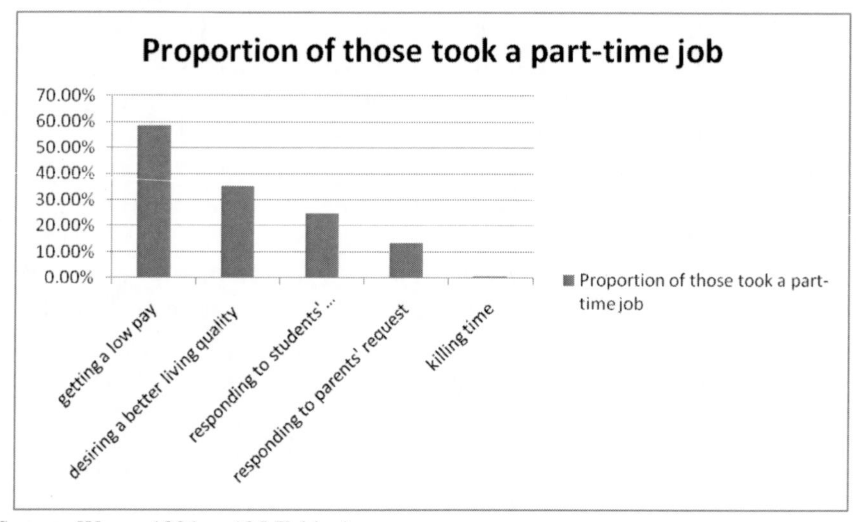

Source: Wong, 1991: p.185 Table 4.

Figure 6.2. The reasons teachers took up a part-time job.

In addition to low pay, private school teachers also worked for an average of two hours longer per day than their public school counterparts. This was substantially a result of class size. The average class size in a public school was twenty; in a private school, it was not uncommon to teach as many as 40 students in a single classroom. Figure 6.3 summarizes the finding by the colonial government on distribution of classes with different sizes in the school year of 1987/1988.

Since the 1999 handover, the Macao SAR government has been investing more and more resources in basic education. One might expect that two consequences of this would be greatly better qualified teachers and a better deal on pay and workload. Indeed, great strides have been made in this area. As mentioned in Chapter 3, a government survey of 888 teachers in 2007 showed that over 90% of private school teachers are now qualified in their position. Specifically, about 70% of teachers now have a higher degree. Table 6.7 (reproducing Table 3.12 in Chapter 3), summarises the distribution of teachers by their qualification.

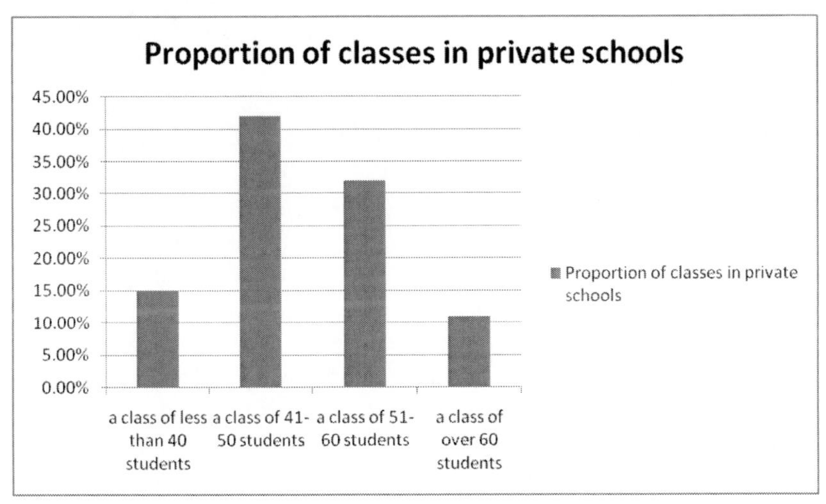

Source: Wong, 1991: p.21.

Figure 6.3. Distribution of classes in private schools in Macao by size.

As described in Chapter 2, class sizes have also been significantly reduced. The Private Legal Frame of 2012 also requires that private schools allocate 70% of their government funding to pay teachers hired, and stipulates a maximum number of teaching hours per week. However, as discussed below, there is still room for principals to manipulate this law against teachers.

Table 6.7. The distribution of private school teachers in Macao in 2007 by qualification

Qualification	Number of teachers	Proportion
Secondary level or below	54	6.08%
Post-secondary diploma	126	14.19%
Sub-degree	62	6.98%
Bachelor's degree	497	55.97%
Post-graduate degree	126	14.19%
Others	23	2.59%
Total	888	100.00%

Source: the website of the DSEJ, a report released in 2007, Chapter 3, p. 27 Table 3-1.

Monitoring

Before the passing of the Private Legal Frame in 2012, private schools had their own patterns of workload assignments to their teaching staff. It was difficult enough to make a comparison across schools with regard to teachers' workload, even when just examining classroom teaching and administrative duties. It should also be highlighted that teachers were asked to perform duties unrelated to teaching, or even unrelated to the school. For instance, teachers were sometimes asked to participate in activities organised by (and for) their school's sponsoring body:

> 'We were asked to call up each parent to vote for a candidate supported by the organization that funded our school in the previous legislative council election. The election was taken place on a Sunday. And I had to get to school and call the parents of every student in my class to campaign for the candidate recommended by the organization that funded our school. (…) It was rather embarrassing but all colleagues were doing that; could I say "No"?' (A teacher, in a focus group interview conducted by the first author)

The Private Legal Frame states more clearly the scope of duties and working hours for private school teachers. While it remains to be seen whether the situation will indeed be improved, the Private Legal Frame at least provides a legal foundation on which teachers' scope of duties can be measured.

In monitoring teachers' performance, however, each private school has its own system of appraisal or evaluation. It is common practice, indeed expected, for teachers to follow the teaching manual designed by their schools, which outline the school's expectations of teachers, their duties, and how they are to be monitored.

Schools of the same type will tend to have similar manuals, so let us take a closer look at these manuals using the four types of school common in Macao. Table 6.8 gives us an overview.

The teacher manuals of public schools are more like a social contract between the SAR government and its teaching staff, stating clearly the entrance requirement and recruitment procedures, outlining the job duties required and the package of pay and benefits, and also making explicit the mechanisms for contract discontinuation.

Table 6.8. Some examples of regulations stated in teacher manuals by school type in Macao

School type	Coverage of teacher manuals	Examples
Government schools	- Rights - Duties - Appointment - Re-appointment and promotion - Evaluation - Pay and benefits (including for overtime work) - Leave - Discontinuation	- Staff are entitled to professional development. - Staff should nurture students to become responsible citizens. - Staff should have the required qualification. - Staff who scored 'good' or above could be reappointed for another year. - It is required to evaluate the performance of staff for the sake of professional development. - The pay of staff is determined by the following formula. - Staff are entitled to an annual leave of 22 days a year. - Staff who violate laws could be subject to formal disciplinary sanction and could also lead to contract discontinuation.
Catholic schools	- Education mission	- Staff should spread the teaching of Catholicism. - Staff should respect students as individuals and their rights to education
Schools run by traditional organizations	- Education mission - Duties - Job description - Pay and benefits - Leave - Appearance	- Staff should love our motherland, Macao, the school, and students. - Staff should complete tasks assigned on time. - Staff should teach about 16 to 18 lessons a week and carry out duties assigned by the school. - The pay of staff should be decided by the principal at the beginning of the school year. - Staff are entitled to 56 days' maternity leave. - Staff should wear uniforms and avoid having unusual hair styles.
Other schools	- Education mission - Arrangements of checking in - Classroom regulation	- Staff should seek to nurture excellent students. - Staff have to check in before 8:00am. - Staff should keep the classroom clean and in order.

By comparison, the teacher manuals of the three other types are derived from their educational missions, religious or otherwise, expecting their teaching staff to behave consistently with such expectations. In addition, the teacher manuals of private schools are more detailed about the required daily routine, such as at what time staff should punch in, and stating what staff should wear and what hairstyle staff should have. What is interesting is that except for the teacher manuals of Catholic schools, teacher manuals are mostly concerned about teachers' appearance and conduct (something observable) rather than the professionalism of teachers. In particular, the teacher manuals of non-Catholic schools rarely mention what educational philosophy or vision is expected of their teaching staff.

It is rarely disputed that a school should have mechanisms of some kind in order to make sure that its teachers' performances live up to the school's expectations; better still, that their performances are up to a professional standard. However, as presented above (and observed by many teachers interviewed by the first author), what most teacher manuals lay out are basically expectations of teachers' appearance and outfit and a few strictures about punctuality and the application procedures for leave. In this sense, the purpose of a school's teacher manuals is more for regulating its teaching staff than for enhancing their professional growth. Nevertheless, many teachers considered it necessary to have teacher manuals for the sake of smooth administration.

> 'Yes, we have our teacher manual. (…) There are many rules and regulations concerning the dress code and our appearance and outfit. (…) In fact, we have our uniforms. School regulations just make clear on which days we should wear formal uniforms and on which days we should wear sports uniforms. (…) I think it is necessary to have such kind of manual. Just as schools have school regulations for students, schools also have teacher manuals for teachers.' (A teacher, in a focus group interview conducted by the first author)

> 'Our school makes it very clear all the rules we have to comply with, such as what time we should check in. (…) But many colleagues are dissatisfied with the practice of asking us to check in after parking our cars.' (A teacher, in a focus group interview conducted by the first author)

In a sense, the majority of teachers in Macao are not drawing a distinction between a sense of professional ethics and conduct specified in a teacher manual of a school. While the latter refers to rules and regulations set up by each school for administrative purposes, the former is about the ethics commonly agreed by the professional community of teachers, which is related to the professionalism of teachers in Macao generally. (We will discuss this further in the next chapter.) What is clear here is that in designing their teacher manuals, private schools are concerned about the image (not necessarily a professional image) of teachers and about whether their teaching staff are compliant in carrying out duties assigned to them. In short, we suspect that the purpose of having a teacher manual is less about enhancing the professionalism of teachers and more about making sure that teachers monitor students in the way the school desires; this could, in turn, boosting the reputation of their schools. This trend becomes even clearer in the appraisal of the teaching staff.

Granted, private schools have legitimate concerns about the delivery of teaching and classroom management. However, in practice, these concerns often drive schools away from their stated educational missions – putting an emphasis on students being cooperative rather than independent, and disciplined (in every sense) rather than curious or interactive. Students are not expected to interact with the teacher in order to learn through discussion, rather they are expected to remain quiet most of the time and to sit properly and listen carefully to the teacher. Under these circumstances, even a teacher who personally favours an interactive style of teaching would find it hard to break away from this sort of conditioning – particularly given the close scrutiny of principals and head teachers. Some teachers explained:

> 'I would like to interact with my students. But the head teacher would come quietly to observe how I teach outside of the classroom on a regular basis. (...) If the head teacher sees that students are not sitting quietly in my lesson, he/she would criticize me after that lesson. (...) Our principal and head teachers want our classes to be in absolute order and silence; an interactive class is considered a failure because I would be failing to control students or to keep my class in order.' (A teacher, personal communication with the first author)

> 'Sure, I know it's better to interact with students. But our principal and head teachers consider a successful class to be a disciplined one, meaning that the class should be in absolute silence.' (A teacher, in a focus group interview conducted by the first author)

> 'In Chinese, the two characters of 'discipline' actually mean control and teaching respectively. That is, to discipline a student, one should get him/her under control first; otherwise, teaching is not possible. (...) Imagine, how can you teach in class where students are talking or not paying attention to you? (...) As I see it, it's necessary to make sure that students are sitting properly and quietly; otherwise, they won't listen to me and they won't learn anything.' (A teacher, in a focus group interview conducted by the first author)

Many teachers mention that their school principals pay attention to whether they can keep their students under control. And authority is indeed a major component of a good teacher. But while order is necessary to deliver of a lesson plan, it is debatable what makes an orderly class. Without doubt, private school teachers have come to a consensus that an orderly class refers to a class of students sitting properly and quietly and thus listening attentively to the teacher. We argue that this idealised picture of a classroom is intended both to inculcate a certain learning style, and to paint a picture of a school that is strict in its discipline – and therefore good. It is not at all clear whether individual teachers buy into this philosophy, for the simple reason that if teachers do not comply, they risk losing their jobs.

The risk of redundancy is real, and nearly constant. Private school teachers in Macao are very rarely tenured, merely employed on rolling contracts that last a year. This fact is perhaps the most crucial in explaining the general quietism of teachers in voicing their own views, or challenging their school principals. Teachers are therefore not really professionals: they are vulnerable employees working to contract. They are subordinate to principals and head-teachers, and are charged only with implementing rules decided from above. Their subordinate position is even clearer when one considers that teachers can be fired for no stated reason, as long as they are paid a month's salary in compensation.

Firing

As in the case of many other employees, in all walks of life, private school teachers will be fired if they violate what is expected of them by their employers (rather than by their professional community). At first glance, it seems reasonable to fire an employee when he/she is not performing or not living up to an expected standard. But there is no law in Macao to govern abuses of this power. There are also no labour unions, and no means to appeal to government. Many teachers say they dare not speak out, lest they be fired just for irritating the principal. There are indeed cases where teachers have been fired for no stated reason. Unsurprisingly, many teachers emphasize that what matters is the principal's judgement: a teacher can make a serious mistake, or break school rules, and still have their contract renewed. On the other hand, a teacher can be fired on the principal's whim, without doing anything wrong.

Here are two examples raised by teachers in some focus group interviews:

> 'Many years ago, a teacher was found to have harassed a female student of his. (...) It was actually reported in newspapers. However, that teacher wasn't fired but could keep his position for some time, because the principal decided not to. (...) And there were no laws or requirements that the principal should fire that teacher. (...) True, in the end the teacher was fired; but he was fired for another mistake he made much later on. (...) I can't remember what the mistake is. (...) But, apparently, the school principal could tolerate that he harassed his student but couldn't accept that he made such mistake.' (A teacher, in a focus group interview conducted by the first author)

> 'A colleague of mine doesn't teach well and always calls in sick. (...) But, the principal likes him a lot and considers that his poor teaching and absences without reason are acceptable. (...) This is so "Macao." The principal makes the decision of re-appointments without being challenged, even by the board. (...) So, you see, what matters to most teachers in contract renewal is not whether they could meet the criteria set by the school, but whether the principal likes them.' (A teacher, in a focus group interview conducted by the first author)

It becomes apparent that private school teachers are not merely closely monitored by the school on a regular basis, but are also under genuine threat of getting fired. This explains why private school teachers do not see themselves as professionals, accountable to their professional community, but vulnerable employees under constant surveillance and threat of being removed. This will be discussed further in the next chapter.

In summary, many private school teachers can be seen as non-professional, if not unqualified, teaching staff. The history of education in colonial Macao has meant that teachers in private schools have tended to be low paid for long hours. This served to make teaching an unattractive career prospect, and in turn necessitated the hiring of unqualified teachers. The social status of teachers in Macao was, and remains, rather low. The Private Legal Frame of 2012 has improved some of these issues at least on the basis of law, but it remains to be seen whether the social standing and pay of teachers increases in future years – particularly while the rest of Macao's economy continues to boom. Teachers in Macao are considered subordinate and dispensable employees. Having hired poorly qualified (or unqualified) staff, private schools in Macao aimed to compensate by closely monitoring their teachers' performance. In the absence of strong labour laws, teachers could be disposed of at the whim of their principal. This describes a vicious circle:

because of limited resources, schools preferred to employ unqualified teachers; to compensate for the teachers' poor qualifications, strict monitoring regimes were put in place; lacking independence, teachers also lack social standing; lacking social standing, the pay and conditions that teachers work under has no incentive to be improved. This vicious circle has not yet been broken.

CONCLUDING REMARKS

In this chapter, we sought to outline the operation of private schools in Macao. We argued that because of the nature of funding to private schools, their ultimate goal is their very survival – through student enrolment. This is because public subsidies to private schools are directly linked to student enrolment at each grade. So private schools compete aggressively to attract students and persuade parents. In the absence of a common academic standard in Macao, the key indicator of a school's success is the conduct and discipline of its students. Private schools will point to the number of students they hold back a grade as evidence of their disciplined approach to education. They will further point to their school regulations as indicating their commitment to certain professional and ethical values.

In practice, private schools actually retain students to make a brand name for their schools. Nobody disputes that private schools need to secure their survival, but we argue that most of these practices are put in place at the expense of students and the quality of education overall. To enforce student discipline, most private schools exert comparably tight controls over their teaching staff.

Teachers are vulnerable waged workers with little job security, and no recourse to appeal should their contracts be terminated. Contracts can be terminated by the single word of a principal, or indeed for no stated reason whatsoever, as long as the teacher is paid a month's salary in compensation. Most teachers simply do what is required of them in order to keep their jobs, rather than upholding a common professional standard or improving their schools through their professional judgements.

We therefore argue that private schools secure their financial stability not only through neglecting the quality of education, but also at the expense of the professionalism of teachers. Not all teachers have been compliant however. We believe that the teaching community in Macao has been going through a process of professional awakening. This is the theme of the next chapter.

Chapter 7

TEACHERS

The quality of education very much depends on the quality of teaching and therefore on the quality of the practitioners – the teachers themselves. As discussed in the previous chapters, because of the chaotic conditions of education under the Portuguese colonial government, teachers in Macao are not considered professionals wider society. Nor are they treated as professionals by their schools. In this chapter, we shall first recapitulate the impact of Macao's colonial history on the work and market conditions for teachers. We shall elaborate on the reasons that teaching fails to attract high-quality candidates; why teachers as a profession are so uniquely vulnerable and effectively voiceless; and why the overall professionalism of teachers in Macao remains open to question. We argue that the vulnerability of teachers with regard to their employers and the wider society necessitates a specific teacher law in Macao. Indeed, something of the sort was achieved by the passing of the Private Legal Frame in 2012. We shall then discuss the changes that the Legal Frame seeks to introduce to the profession of teaching in Macao, and its potential impact on the professionalism of teachers. The Legal Frame follows several years of demonstrations by teachers in Macao for greater professional recognition and job security; several of these demonstrations in recent years could be taken to mark the beginnings of a political awakening for teachers in Macao.

Thirdly, therefore, we shall discuss this apparent political and professional awakening, particularly among private schools teachers. We shall make special reference to the establishment of a teacher-led initiative to promote and codify the 'ethics' of teaching in Macao.

HISTORICAL LEGACY OF COLONIALISM ON THE PROFESSIONALISM OF TEACHERS

As we have mentioned in previous chapters, the education of the local Chinese community was not a priority for the Portuguese colonial government in Macao. Where private schools were set up to address the needs of the Chinese population, they were largely ineligible for government funds, which meant that most such private schools could not afford qualified teachers. This has had direct consequences for the professionalism of teacher's in Macao today: both in terms of their formal qualifications and fitness to teach, and in terms of the vulnerability of their jobs due to a lack of provable professionalism. Until very recently, this also stopped teachers from banding together to make their voices heard. All negotiations about teachers' employment packages and professional development tended to involve the government and the heads of schools, bypassing teachers entirely. This legacy remains a hindrance to the professional development of teachers. Let us look first at the work and market situations of teachers before the passing of the Legal Frame in 2012.

The Work and Market Situations of Teachers

According to Max Weber's well-known ideas, commonly summarized in introductory textbooks of Sociology (cf. Giddens, 2006), work situation and market situation are two sociological concepts that allow us to differentiate the treatments of various groups of employees – particularly between the relatively advantaged middle class (e.g., professionals, managers, and administrators) and the relatively disadvantaged working class (e.g., manual labourers of differing skill levels). Work situation refers to the autonomy and self-direction that employees enjoy in their jobs, and market situation refers to the rewards of various types (such as money and social standing), that employees obtain from their jobs. Following this distinction, we seek to depict the competing situations of private school teachers in Macao during the colonial period and to argue that private school teachers were not treated as professionals, lacking advantages that an equivalent post in the West could confer.

While the colonial Portuguese only took care of the education of the Portuguese and their children by running public schools, the education for the local Chinese was shouldered by private schools run by various types of sponsoring bodies. As a result, there was a huge gap in resources between public schools and private schools. Unsurprisingly therefore, there was also a huge gap in pay and benefits between teachers hired by public schools and their private school counterparts. Small wonder that private school teaching was considered a low-paid job; smaller wonder still that private school teachers had to supplement their low wages with other incomes – as mentioned by many retired teachers interviewed by the second author (see Chapter 4). As mentioned in Chapter 6, in 1987/88, on average, private school teachers earned MOP2,500 to MOP3,500 a month, whereas their public school counterparts made MOP8,000 to MOP10,000 each month (with fourteen months' salaries a year). Apart from that, public school teachers and private school teachers also differ in workload. Despite getting much higher pay and having many more benefits, public school teachers usually taught classes of small size and worked for much shorter working hours than their private school counterparts. As also mentioned in Chapter 6, where the average class-size in a 1980s public school was about 20 students, it was around 40 to 50 students for private schools. Furthermore, the number of working hours per week and the mechanisms for compensating overtime were stated very clearly in the contracts of public school teachers. No such stipulations were made in the contracts of private school teachers. As will be discussed in greater depth below, private school teachers had weak bargaining power with regard to schools and/or principals.

Where each school was effectively a world into itself, there was usually not much room for negotiation. Similarly, because of the diversity of sponsoring bodies running schools and their finances, the pay, benefits and workload of private school teachers varied massively across schools. Most sponsoring bodies had very tight finances and could not therefore afford to offer particularly attractive terms and pay to teachers. In a private interview with a teacher (a former student of hers) in 2010, the first author was told that pay was so low (under MOP8,000 per month) that he had been forced to take up two teaching jobs: one in a day school and another in an evening school. The need among private schools to keep costs low also extended to their enrolment of students. Put simply, they enrolled as many as they could, which meant that low-paid teachers were required to teach very big classes. In some cases, to further minimise cost, private schools even asked teachers to teach subjects outside their usual expertise (see Chapter 6). While it is usually more difficult to teach a large class than a small one, it certainly takes more preparation time per class, and more time to grade students throughout the school year. Even in the case of very good teachers, the sheer number of students meant that it was very difficult to concentrate on the academic needs of individual students, let alone their emotional and social needs.

Private school teachers were very closely monitored within individual schools, but not assessed at all outside of their school. The result was that while almost every aspect of a teacher's performance and appearance was constantly under scrutiny, there was no countervailing view of teachers as a profession. This remains to some extent true of Macao today, as a number of our interviewees expressed:

> 'Head teachers or higher-ranking administrators would do the patrolling every day. (…) Yet they don't come into our classrooms. They would just walk pass or stand outside of the classroom. (…) What concerns them most is whether students are quiet in classes.' (A teacher, personal communication with the first author)

> 'Most principals are concerned about whether students are performing rather than learning. (…) And the major indicator of a good class used by most principals is whether the class is quiet. (…) It's rather difficult to have an interactive class in Macao.' (A teacher, in a focus group interview conducted by the first author)

In other words, because of their diverse qualifications, private school teachers were usually not trusted professionally. Rather more ironically, the head teachers, higher ranking administrators and principals in private schools monitored the teaching but were not necessarily qualified teachers themselves. In general, the concern of such administrators was not the quality of teaching or students' quality of learning, but the efficiency of delivery: a quiet and thus disciplined classroom. The idea that a disciplined classroom is an ideal classroom remains an ingrained teaching ideal in Macao.

In addition to the duties of teaching and grading and administration, it was not uncommon for private school teachers to be asked to carry out tasks for their sponsoring bodies, although those tasks were not related to the schools. This might, for instance, involve doing some promotion activities for the sponsoring bodies. Indeed, as mentioned in Chapter 6, this still goes on: with teachers being instructed, for instance, to call up parents to vote for a candidate supported by their sponsoring body in a Legislative Council election. An outsider might well wonder why private school teachers do not say 'no' to such requests. This brings us to perhaps the single most important aspect of the market situation of private school teachers: they are no different from many other waged workers in Macao.

Pay and benefits to teachers has historically been low in Macao; as mentioned in Chapter 6, wages were sometimes lower than those of a manual worker. Indeed, the total income of teachers was usually their monthly salary plus a number of allowances derived from other activities. For instance, it was common to pay private school teachers for after-school tutorials (teaching the same students they had seen earlier in the day) or for summer classes (despite the academic year ending in June; schools sometimes required student to return in July and early August). "Outstanding" teachers also sometimes received extra remuneration from particularly generous schools – if, for instance, a teacher was held to have particularly good punctuality. (It is not unheard of for teachers to have attendance cards punched every morning, afternoon, and evening.) Teachers were therefore paid wages, rather than salaries, calculated in terms of the number of tasks performed. And, some generous schools would give some compensatory amount of money at the end of a calendar year to outstanding teachers; one criterion for judging whether a teacher was performing well was punctuality. The colonial Portuguese government did not have any regulatory oversight of this situation; neither did it have centralized oversight of the pay and working hours of private school teachers. The only difference between a teacher and another waged employee was, therefore, the hiring agent.

Moreover, private schools abided by the same minimal labour laws that governed the private sector throughout Macao. This meant that teachers could be fired at their boss's whim. As long as a principal gave a month's wages in compensation, the law allowed for any employee to be immediately fired. In addition, it was common to offer teachers a contract of only a single academic year: teachers therefore were constantly under threat of being fired. In the absence of trade unions in Macao generally, and a teachers' union in particular, there was no body teachers could turn to if they felt they were being treated unfairly. This all comes together to create a scene in which teachers were reluctant to say no to any request from a school or its funders, no matter how apparently unreasonable or outside the scope of their job and training.

While the colonial Portuguese government basically ignored the practices of private schools, including those related to the welfare of private school teachers, minimal financial assistance from the government was observed from the late 1970s onwards. Private school teachers began to receive small direct subsidies from the colonial government for the first time in 1977, and began to receive indirect subsidies in the form of tax exemption since 1984. These minimal subsidies improved the immediate lot of teachers, but could not necessarily be said to have put teachers on to the road to formal, recognised "professionalism", nor to have improved their social standing. Indeed, it is generally felt in Macao that teaching is a matter of voluntary sacrifice, and that people who become teachers should not expect a decent salary or benefits. On the whole, teachers in Macao are a lot less well respected than their counterparts in the West.

Low morale among teachers has been exacerbated in recent years by the boom in Macao's GDP, much of it built on the liberalisation of gambling laws in 2004. As a result of this boom, the wages of people involved in the gaming industries (such as dealers and croupiers) as well as those in ancillary trade (such as waiters and bar staff) have been constantly on the rise. In many cases, the wages of gaming staff have now outstripped those of teachers in private schools. In our interviews with teachers, it was not uncommon to come across anecdotes and scenarios such as this:

> 'A colleague of mine told me about this. The other day, he wanted to convince his students that it was necessary to study hard by posing a rhetorical question to his class: "What else could you do if you don't have a qualification? Do you want to become a beggar?" (...) This is rather cheesy and many teachers have done that before. (...) Yet, one student stood up and challenged him: "I don't need a qualification. When I get to 18, I can become a dealer and will earn more than you. How much do you earn now? And how dare you to criticize us like this? What's the use of being a teacher?" (...) My colleague was flattened and felt humiliated. (...) But that's the reality facing teachers in Macao: no one respects us.'
> (A teacher, personal communication with the first author)

In fact, the idea of teachers as not being a professional body was a common self-image described by in-service teachers taught by the first author at the University of Macau: it was not just that they were not treated as professionals by their schools and the wider society; they often did not think of themselves as professionals either, and pointed to their undignified, meagre wages as proof. In contrast to teachers in private schools, when public school teachers met the entrance requirement set by the government, they were instantly considered civil servants, enjoying not merely an attractive reward package but also a high social standing in Macao.

It could be argued that the disciplinarian tendencies of private schools guaranteed at least some professionalism among otherwise unqualified teachers. But this still served to undermine the basic professionalism of individual teachers, and of teaching as a profession. Add to this the tight budgets of most private schools, and you had a situation in which most of the people who applied for a teaching post were unqualified to teach. This created a vicious circle: small budgets necessitated the hiring of unqualified teachers; unqualified teachers necessitated close monitoring by school management; this close monitoring served to undermine teachers, without necessarily giving them any incentive to improve their teaching performance. While private schools themselves were granted a high degree of autonomy in Macao, teachers in those schools had almost no autonomy whatsoever. In a situation where the professional development of teachers was neglected due to cost, the ability of such teachers to provide a decent education is clearly called into question.

The Professionalism of Private School Teachers

There are several common criteria of professionalism (e.g., Ingersoll and Perda, 2008): a license to practice (e.g., a recognized entrance requirement); professional knowledge, professional autonomy and therefore self-governance; and a relatively high social standing. Using these criteria, let us take a look at the practices of teaching in private schools in Macao in order to gauge the professionalism of private school teachers.

While public school teachers in Macao were required to have a specific qualification before entering the classroom, this was not the case for private school teachers. Many trainee and in-service teachers told the first author that before the passing of the Private Legal Frame in 2012, anyone could become a teacher in Macao, as long as a principal was willing to hire you. This view is not absolutely legally correct, but it is consistent with personal observation and even with some relevant statistics. In the 1980s, for instance, about half of teachers in Macao were not qualified teachers. This was partly to do with the underdevelopment of higher education in general (Bray, 2002), and teacher training in particular, throughout Macao. Even where a major teacher training institute was established (specifically, the University of Macau), it did not open until 1990. Before this point, there were no teacher training programmes at a university level in Macao. This is unsurprising given the general isolation of education for the local Chinese in Macao in the 1950s and 60s. Where the population as a whole were under-educated, it was rare enough for a teacher in a private school to even have a secondary qualification, let alone a higher degree. Even when secondary qualifications became more common, a teacher was more often selected on the basis of their subject knowledge, rather than any skill or qualification in pedagogy or the ethics of teaching.

The situation has improved greatly since 1999. A 2007 DSEJ survey showed that of a sample of 888 private school teachers, 497 had a bachelor's degree, and 126 had a post-graduate degree. In all, around 70% of the teachers surveyed had met the level of educational attainment required to become a teacher. This, however, is "qualification" for teaching in only the most technical sense. It still leans very much on evidence of personal educational attainment and subject knowledge; it does not necessarily stress the skills involved in teaching itself – a general sense of professional ethics as well as pedagogical practice. Very often, the professional judgement of teachers is effectively subsumed by the code of conduct of the institution they happen to teach in, rather than to a general sense of what is required by the profession.

Yet qualification is not the whole story of guaranteeing the quality of teaching. Teaching is a profession requiring not just subject knowledge, but pedagogical knowledge and professional ethics. With such professional knowledge, teachers are expected to be able to make professional judgements, in that their judgements are accountable to the teaching profession, rather than simply accountable to the teaching institution that employs them. Because of this sense of wider responsibility, professionals tend to enjoy a very high level of autonomy that allows them to govern the hiring and practices of their own kind. However, this description simply did not fit the case of Macao at all during the colonial era: to reiterate, most teachers were unqualified to teach. There is reason to believe that situation has not changed dramatically nowadays.

This view can be seen from the ratings on the professionalism of teachers in Macao reported in the 2007 survey (funded by the DSEJ). To illustrate, let us summarise some of its major findings about private school teachers. 888 private school teachers randomly selected in Macao were assessed in this survey in respect of five areas: professional spirit, professional ideals, professional knowledge, professional capability, and awareness of the development of professional autonomy. The survey summarised that private school teachers in Macao scored somewhere in the upper middle in all five domains. Their scores in the five domains could be ranked in a descending order as follows. They scored highest in the domain of professional spirit, then professional knowledge, then professional ideals, then awareness of the development of professional autonomy, and lowest in the domain of professional capability. Despite their scores, five points are of concern and deserve a lot of our attention where the professionalism of teachers and the quality of education in Macao is concerned.

The first is about professional spirit. Most teachers show that they love students; yet, generally speaking teachers in Macao respect the teaching profession but do not enjoy it. The second is about professional knowledge. While 60% to 70% teachers in Macao have a reasonably good professional knowledge in their fields, most teachers seem inadequate in integrating pedagogical knowledge and educational philosophy (including rationales behind student assessments) in their practices. The third concern is about professional ideals. Where most teachers are confident that they can help students with learning difficulties make improvements, teachers in Macao in general fail to appreciate the individuality (or diversity) and potential of students. Pedagogically speaking, teachers in Macao place too much emphasis on transmitting basic knowledge and skills to students to an extent that they gloss over how to nurture and develop students to acquire an initiative towards learning, problem-solving abilities, and intellectual independence. How this translates to pedagogical practices in classroom is in a didactic teaching approach: only 34% of teachers regularly arrange for class activities to facilitate students' exploration and cooperative learning, and a significant majority admit that they are used to lecturing alone in the classroom. The fourth concern is about professional capability: while teachers score lowest in professional capability out of the five domains, the two items scored the lowest are their reflexivity and research ability. Specifically, about 60% of teachers do not reflect on their teaching. This is rather alarming. Reflexivity allows teachers to learn from their experiences; without reflexivity, an experienced teacher could have just repeated his/her mistakes again and again. The fifth is about awareness of the development of professional autonomy. While this awareness is a driving force for teachers' life-long professional development, most teachers in Macao do not have a clear idea of professional development and some are simply lack such awareness altogether.

In short, the professionalism of the existing team of private school teachers in Macao is still of concern. Furthermore, as expected against the general background of education in Macao, private school teachers are not generally involved in designing either curriculum or assessment. Rather, they were merely expected to carry out technical tasks such as teaching a particular curriculum and assessing students in a particular way designed by their schools. Similarly, in private schools at least, teachers were rarely involved professionally in a recruitment committee to hire new teaching staff. Appointments of new hires were usually decided by individual principals, sometimes alone. Given the prevailing labour law in Macao, teachers are never asked to provide professional judgements about whether the practices of private school teachers are unprofessional or unethical, let alone allowed to participate in decisions as to whether individual private school teachers should be fired.

Professional malpractices were simply not an issue and the firing of teachers was in most cases decided by individual principals. In short, instead of giving professional judgments, private school teachers are expected to simply take order from their senior administrators. In fact, given their vulnerability, private school teachers usually dared not voice opinions of any sort, let alone opinions that expressed grievance or discontent.

All these factors contribute to the fact that private-school teachers in Macao do not enjoy a high social standing. This has become particularly pointed since the general wages in Macao – and particularly those of people in the gaming industry – have gone on a drastic rise. Lacking autonomy as a profession, or support from senior management in individual schools, it is little wonder that a particular image of the teacher prevails in Macao. That image is of somebody who is prepared to make sacrifices, and who should not complain about those sacrifices thereafter.

Unless somebody is seen as having a particular vocation calling towards teaching, it is unlikely their parents or friends would recommend they join the profession. This issue of the social standing of teachers points in its own way towards the necessity of a teacher law in Macao, if both the standing of the profession in general and the quality of teaching in particular were to be improved. A teacher law was indeed passed in 2012, so let us look at the improvements it might make.

THE PASSING OF 'THE PRIVATE LEGAL FRAME'

A teacher law in Macao – the 'Private Legal Frame' (Law 3/2012) – was passed in 2012. Its legal aim is to seek to upgrade the career security and the professional quality of teachers hired by private schools in Macao. For the present purposes, we shall focus on four areas to see how far this teacher law can bring improvements to the treatment of private school teachers in Macao. The four are: pay and career progression, workload and working hours, entrance requirements, and appraisal and professional development.

Major Focus of the 'Private Legal Frame'

As a result of Macao's colonial past, and the consequent development of private education for the native Chinese population, there has never been much regulation of the pay and conditions of private-school teachers in Macao. In general, the teachers have been badly paid and enjoyed a social status to match. The Private Legal Frame specifies that 70% of all government subsidies should go towards teachers' salaries, and furthermore that this basic salary should amount to the majority of their overall pay. In addition, these teachers are now entitled to a monetary award based on their seniority in the organization, and their pension.

More importantly, the Private Legal Frame also requires that private schools to set up a career ladder for their teaching staff according to seniority, so as to make sure that there is an increment in pay over the years. It is true that this regulation on pay does not immediately close the gap in pay between public school teachers and their private school counterparts; but it at least makes it illegal for private schools to underpay their teaching staff. It therefore recognises the contribution of experienced teachers and may help narrow the gap in teachers' pay between private schools.

In addition to being paid badly, private school teachers have basically been required to do whatever their school principals asked them to without getting extra pay. While it was not surprising that teachers did not get paid for teaching overtime, it was also not uncommon for teachers to be asked to do tasks irrelevant to teaching or education or even their schools in general. This is no longer the case. The Private Legal Frame states that teachers should work for 36 hours a week in all, even if that work is non-teaching related. The Private Legal Frame goes further, in stating how many lessons are to be taught by each teacher at different levels. For example, a secondary school teacher is required to teach 16-18 lessons a week, a primary school teacher 18-20 lessons, and a kindergarten teacher 21 to 23 lessons. There is also a special calculation for teachers teaching in special schools and evening schools. The Private Legal Frame also makes clear that teachers can be assigned non-teaching tasks but they should be related to education or to the school, and that teachers should be paid for overtime work, be it teaching or non-teaching. In this way, such arrangements serve to protect the interests of teachers and provide room for teachers to focus on teaching rather than tasks irrelevant to education.

While the Private Legal Frame focuses considerably on the pay and benefits and rights of private school teachers, it also makes room for discussing their duties, especially insuring their professionalism. To this end, the Private Legal Frame sets out clearly the entrance requirements for teachers at different levels. As discussed above (as well as in Chapter 6), the qualification of private school teachers varies a lot and many of them are technically unqualified. This has been one fundamental reason that private school teachers in Macao are not treated as professionals. Now clear entrance requirements are set for qualified teachers at different levels. For example, teachers hired by kindergartens should have at least a qualification of higher education in pre-primary education, or have at least a qualification in higher education and a teacher training education in pre-primary education recognized by the DSEJ. In the past, anyone could be hired as a teacher as long as a principal agreed to hire him/her; in stark contrast, it is now clear that only qualified teachers are eligible. This should function as a guarantee for the quality of teaching in later years.

Reinforcing this, the Private Legal Frame details mechanisms of appraisal for teachers (as well as mechanisms of appeal on behalf of teachers who feel they have been mistreated). In addition, the Private Legal Frame requires teachers to take a number of hours per year of in-service training or professional development. This practice seeks to make sure that teachers keep pace with societal development, further enhancing the professionalism of teachers.

Implementation of the Private Legal Frame

In short, the passing of 'the Private Legal Frame' seeks to offer teachers a package attracting qualified teachers to join the teaching profession on the one hand, and to make room for teachers to become more professional on the other. In other words, it seeks to encourage the professionalism of teachers by treating them as professionals, thereby improving the quality of education they can provide. There are loopholes in the law, however, which certain private schools seem keen to take advantage of.

For instance, schools are now obliged to pay senior teachers at least 1.3 times what they pay junior teachers. Some schools get around this by forcing the most senior teachers to retire. Similarly, while 70% of all subsidies to private schools are now legally required to go towards teachers' pay, few schools are as transparent in their accounting as is ideal. Teachers therefore cannot say they are being paid the correct amount. With regard to teachers' workload, while it is required that teachers should work for a certain number of hours a week, some schools discount non-teaching tasks from their calculations, such as attending meetings. Equally, while schools are now forbidden from asking teachers to take up irrelevant tasks, schools can reframe these tasks to look as though they have something to do with teaching.

Against this background, teachers are still reluctant to speak out. This is partly because the Private Legal Frame does not reform Macao's general labour laws, leaving teachers vulnerable to immediate dismissal. Likewise, in the absence of a committed trade union for teachers, those who do feel victimised have no voice to speak for them. As a result, teachers remain essentially subordinate and vulnerable.

There are further questions as to how much the Private Legal Frame can really affect the professionalism of teachers. The Legal Frame sets up entrance requirements at each stage of education, insists on consistent mechanisms of appraisal, and forces schools to allow teachers time for professional development. However, what it cannot do is dismiss teachers in post who are not qualified to teach. Such teachers are, unsurprisingly, resistant to the idea of annual appraisals. They are equally resistant to taking courses to further their professional development (an opinion voiced to the first author in several personal communications). The hope of change in the system is therefore placed almost entirely on new recruits.

But here we reach a demographic problem. As demonstrated in Table 7.1, the Macau Office of Higher Education is predicting a shortfall of 700 teachers (at all levels) in forthcoming years. While the Private Legal Frame provides for in-service training and professional development, it cannot increase the number of teacher training courses and colleges, let alone assess the effectiveness of particular teacher training courses.

Table 7.1. Forecast of teachers demanded made by the Macau Office of Higher Education

	Teachers demanded	Teachers supplied
Accumulated number estimated until 2015	1,406-1,548	802
Annual average	352-387	201

Source: the DSEJ website.

Demographics also plays its part in making teaching an unattractive profession. Wages in the gaming industry (and in industries that are supported by it) are set to rise exponentially, meaning that the only way to address the shortfall of qualified teachers is likely to be the continued recruitment of unqualified teachers.

Remarks on the Private Legal Frame

Undoubtedly, the Private Legal Frame is meant to enhance the professionalism of teachers. It focuses on improving their reward package (thereby attracting more ambitious candidates) and boosting the training of teachers (thereby improving educational standards on the whole). The workload of teachers is on the whole more balanced.

Some schools still find loopholes in order not to comply with the law; and the law does not on its own immediately narrow the gap between the salaries and terms of those in private schools versus those of their counterparts in public schools; but it does pave the way for gradual and complete compliance. However, the law does not address the fundamental conditions of labour relations in Macao. While teachers are now required to have professional qualifications and to receive ongoing training and appraisal, they remain as vulnerable as they ever were. Teachers, furthermore, can resist centralized requirements if they do not feel they have job security. However, the Private Legal Frame is undoubtedly a valuable formal contract between the government and teachers, seeking to enhance the professionalism of teachers for everyone's benefit.

The quality of education on offer remains in doubt, but we should wait to see how effective the Private Legal Frame is in combatting the legacy of colonial education in Macao. While private school teachers have either been treated as victims exploited by schools (vulnerable waged workers rather than autonomous professionals) or been seen as unqualified practitioners ruining the education of students, the effort of private school teachers has often been overlooked in fighting for the passing of the Private Legal Frame. This then brings us to the political awakening of private school teachers in Macao.

The Political and Professional Awakening of Teachers

Private school teachers in Macao could once in general have been considered politically apathetic. There were at least two reasons for that. The first is that teachers were engaged in an oppressive relationship with their schools. As was discussed above, as well as in Chapter 6, given the colonial legacy most private school teachers were unqualified. Besides, given that their working relationship with the school was circumscribed by the labour law, private school teachers were treated as no different from any other vulnerable waged employee. As long as a school provided a teacher with a required amount of compensation, the school could fire the teacher without necessarily giving a reason. It was true that under this circumstance in the West, the teacher would have turned to a labour union to sue the school; but, in Macao, it was perfectly legal for the school to do that to the teacher. In actuality, there were (and are) no formal organizations that private school teachers could turn to. The second reason for the political apathy of private school teachers in Macao is a culture of political participation through associations, as is discussed in Chapter 3. And in the field of education, during the colonial era, the power struggle between the Chinese and the colonial Portuguese government over educational issues had been taken place via the platform of associations, specifically associations in the field of education. Essentially the following three associations were the largest associations in education in scale (in terms of the number of their members and also the scale of their organizations): the Chinese Educators Association of Macau (whose member schools are usually schools run by traditional organizations), the Union of Catholic Schools of Macau (whose member schools are the Catholic Church), and Associação Educativa da Função Pública de Macau. These associations were usually run by school principals.

Take the Chinese Educators Association of Macau as an example. As indicated in Table A7.1, even in 2013, out of 29 core members, 14 were school principals or vice principals and 7 were head teachers (who were more administrators than teachers in the case of Macao) and 2 were associate professors (from universities). Only 6 were frontline teachers. In brief, while teachers' benefits may well be fought for by such associations on behalf of teachers, there were no teachers' voices in such struggles in the colonial era. Rather, school principals were fighting against the colonial Portuguese government for the general benefit of the education of the Chinese. After the 1999 handover, however, the regulators and managers of private schools have found it difficult to accept that their interest might be at odds with those of an explicitly pro-Chinese government. As a result, teachers do not quite know how much to lobby government, lest their rewards be handed directly to the schools (e.g., Macao Daily, 25 February 2008).

As an example, after the 1999 handover, given a drastic increase in resources invested in basic education in Macao, private schools had been receiving an increasing amount of subsidies from the Macao SAR government. However, despite this increase, before the passing of the Private Legal Frame, the pay of private school teachers had not been improved much. Small wonder that private school teachers had been urging the Macao SAR government to implement mechanisms to monitor the allocation of resources from the Macao SAR government by private schools (e.g., Chan, 2010). In brief, both at a school level and at the public level, in the colonial era and even after the handover private school teachers did not have much room for political participation with regard to fighting for improving their pay and benefits or upgrading their professional status.

Two Important Teachers' Demonstrations After the 1999 Handover

Be that as it may, lacking political platforms for teachers' voices or political participation somehow explained why most private school teachers in Macao are politically apathetic; nevertheless, this does not mean that private school teachers are willingly fatalistic about such plight. It was not uncommon to hear private school teachers' grievances and complaints, albeit privately. While it is not usual for private school teachers to voice out their discontent publicly, their discontent has been brewing and ultimately reaches a point of serving as a trigger for their own political awakening. Indeed, after the end of the monopoly of the gambling industry in 2004, the economy of Macao has been performing extraordinarily well. While quite a considerably proportion of people in Macao are reaping such economic benefits, ordinary people actually cannot really share much from such an economic boom; private school teachers are one of those who bitterly feel that they are being slighted and their interests are not being taken care of. In particular, when lowly educated dealers can earn such a handsome salary, some private school teachers who have been working so hard are still making such a meagre income that could barely make their ends meet. This shameful wage gap, as it were, indeed drew a group of about 50 teachers to take to the streets in 2007 (Macao Daily, 3 December 2007). Despite this so-called small scale demonstration, its social meaning should be understood against the context of the so-called harmonious political environment in Macao: in general there are not many demonstrations in Macao and usually demonstrations are organised by the grassroots against illegal labour, as indicated in Table A7.2. In addition, private school teachers are usually so low profile in making themselves heard either at school or in public. So the 2007 demonstration of 50 teachers (not even widely reported) is a wake-up call to the SAR government that much more needs to be done for private-school teachers if the quality of education in Macao is to be improved.

The 2007 demonstration could be regarded as a demarcation point in the history of fighting for the pay and benefits of private-school teachers. This demonstration, together with the general chronic disappointment of private school teachers that 'the Private Legal Frame' was still under discussion, has made more private school teachers feel more of the need for having a teacher law in Macao if the work and market situations are to be improved and the professional status of teachers is to be enhanced. And this somehow could be seen as a prelude to a subsequent demonstration on a much larger scale in 2011. The 2011 demonstration was initiated by three young teachers who were reading the same post-graduate programme at the time. The following information is from an interview with two of them by the first author. Given the chronic discontent among private school teachers, what triggered this demonstration was an announcement of an increase in teachers' direct subsidies and annual rewards in 15 April 2011: the extent of the increase was 7% and 15% respectively but in monetary terms the increase in direct subsidies was only MOP300 (for teachers with teacher training) and MOP140 (for teachers without teacher training) and the increase in annual rewards was MOP30. At the time, while the starting point of pay for public school teachers was MOP27,280, on average the pay of private school teachers was about MOP17,000 (including subsidies of all kinds from the SAR government). Unsurprisingly, most private school teachers considered the actual monetary increase in direct subsidies and annual rewards insulting and were also accused the SAR government of masking the truth by directing the public to focus on the extent of increase – 7% and 15% respectively – but glossing over the fact that the basic amount of the subsidies had been very small over the years. This incidence aroused a more general discussion in public about the plight of private school teachers again (Macao Daily, 16 May 2011a). Within days, a forum on the internet had received responses from hundreds and hundreds of private school teachers (several teachers, through personal communication with the first author). And the three young teachers sought to organize a demonstration on the 1st of May so as to take the issue to a higher level and to the light of the public.

Two of the three young teachers told the first author that the DSEJ reacted very fast: they contacted the three young teachers and then arranged for a private discussion with representatives from various associations and a small group of private school teachers led by the three young teachers over the chronic plight of private school teachers in Macao (Macao Daily, 2 May 2011). Under great political pressure, the DSEJ sought to calm down private school teachers through this arrangement in the hope that a large-scale teachers' demonstration on the 1st of May could have been avoided. Yet, a lot more private-school teachers seemed to be aroused, waking up to the fact that they had been under-paid and over-worked (Macao Daily, 2 May 2011; Macao Daily, 3 May 2011; Macao Daily, 16 May 2011b).

Nevertheless, it did not seem appealing to the public if teachers gathered together for a demonstration simply for the sake of MOP300. This reason did not seem to give much political legitimation to the planned demonstration. Therefore, in organising for the demonstration, the three young teachers sought to appeal to political and professional awakening of private school teachers in Macao, conveying a message to private school teachers that there was a pressing need for improving the situation of private school teachers if Macao really cared about the quality of its next generations. And so, the focus of their demonstration was shifted to the fact that the work and market situations of private school teachers in Macao were not comparable to their western counterparts, and that private school teachers did not enjoy much professional status in Macao and their concern about the long-term development of education in Macao.

In organizing for the demonstration, the three young teachers sought to maximize the involvement of private school teachers; they organized a number of mass meetings with frontline teachers so as to discuss educational issues, particularly the chronic plight of teachers in Macao. Finally, after discussions after discussions, eight goals were incorporated in the following slogans in this demonstration: delaying no more to pass 'the Private Legal Frame,' creating a fair platform for communication between teachers and the SAR government, overseeing the effective use of public funding in education, making a reasonably increase in funding allocated to education, upgrading the professional status of teachers, paving the way for the stable development of the teaching profession, implementing courses for the professional development of teachers, and participating in the ten-year educational plan for Macao.

Perhaps we cannot be sure if teachers joined the demonstration out of agreeing on such noble goals; and we would not rule out the possibility that teachers joined the demonstration out of their concern about MOP300 subsidies. Yet, given that there were 5,104 teachers in Macao (counted until

2010), more than 500 teachers joined this demonstration, which outnumbered demonstrations organised by other associations on the same day, when 2300 people in total took to the streets on 1 May 2011 (Macao Daily, 2 May 2011). The 2011 demonstration was turned to be so far the greatest scale of teachers' demonstration in Macao. And it indeed attracted a lot of public concern that somehow put the Macao SAR government under pressure to respond to the requests raised in this demonstration. Together with the accumulated effect of continuous effort made by so many teachers since the colonial era, we could say that the 2011 demonstration somehow accentuated the passing of 'the Private Legal Frame' (Macao Daily, 19 March 2012)

Setting Professional Ethics for Teachers in Macao

Despite the success of this stage of struggle for a better position of private school teachers, this success does not automatically improve the professional status of teachers in Macao. After all, as is found in the 2007 survey discussed above, the majority of the existing team of teachers do not see the importance of the professionalism of teachers and they are not conscious of making professional development. Besides, given the chronic unprofessionalism of teachers, the general public are not so sympathetic with the plight teachers and do not see teachers as professionals or the need for passing the Private Legal Frame. Yet, one of the slogans voiced out in the 2011 demonstration is about the professionalism of teachers and their professional development. In response, the Chinese Educators Association of Macau took the initiative and invited the other two major associations in education so as to form a task force (constituted by educators as well as some frontline teachers) to work on this area in the hope that their collective effort in bettering the education in Macao could be sustained. Consequently, the Chinese Educators Association of Macau cooperated with Associação Educativa da Função Pública de Macau to form a task force on setting professional ethics for teachers in Macao (Macao Daily, 29 May 2013). Perhaps because of political dynamics in the field of education, the Union of Catholic Schools of Macau did not respond to this initiative or join this task force (however, it initiated another similar task force much later on). The task force was formed mainly by frontline teachers and some local researchers in education in Macao, including the second author. In short, the task force on setting professional ethics for teachers in Macao pledged to promote the importance of self-governance to frontline teachers and seek to collect opinions from individual frontline teachers in order to set up a code of professional ethics. Through this collective effort initiated by this group of frontline teachers, a professional community could be formed with a consensus on the underlying principles governing their professional practices. Therefore, if this social movement from the bottom, so to speak, is to succeed, then it could be seen as a manifestation of teachers' empowerment.

Given his position in this task force, the second author provided detailed information about the operation of the task force. In order to see whether there is a consensus among frontline teachers on the necessity for setting up professional ethics for teachers in Macao, the task force invited Dr. Wai-Bing Yu, an expert from Hong Kong, to speak for a seminar open to frontline teachers, including students enrolling in teacher training programmes in April 2012. And it was planned to ask attendees to fill out questionnaires on the necessity for setting up teachers' professional ethics in Macao at the end of the seminar. About 400 people attended the seminar and 113 questionnaires were collected. Out of the 113 collected questionnaires, 93.8% considered that it was necessary to set up such professional ethics for teachers in Macao. On this basis, the task force started to make effort to construct a code of professional ethics particular to Macao. What they did was to examine the professional code of ethics for teachers found in Britain (set by the National Union of Teachers), the USA (set by the National Education Association), and Taiwan (set by the National Teachers' Association) so as to see which professional ethics would also be applicable to Macao. From this examination, about 30 professional ethics were selected to constitute a blueprint for further consultation. Turning this blueprint into promotional pamphlets (with questionnaires) distributed to frontline workers, the task force sought to consult frontline workers openly for two months (May and June 2012) in order to collect their views on the selected professional ethics.

During the two-month open consultation, the task force arranged for four mass meetings: three were arranged for frontline teachers and one for the public; there were about 250 number of attendance. Apart from such large-scale open consultation meetings, the task force also visited eight individual schools to organize specific seminars for teachers of those schools; and there were about 1,000 number of attendance. After sending out 5,000 promotional pamphlets (with questionnaires) to collect views of frontline teachers on the 30 selected professional ethics for two months, the task force collected 1,527 questionnaires. 1,444 out of the collected questionnaires were valid: 87.63% agreed on the necessity for setting up professional ethics for teachers in Macao but 12.37% disagreed. While each respondent was asked to rank whether each of the 30 selected professional ethics was appropriate for Macao, the task force decided only to include those professional ethics if there were over two-thirds (66.67%) of respondents who ranked that that particular ethics was appropriate for Macao; 11 professional ethics were selected and were listed in Table 7.2.

Table 7.2. The selected professional ethics gaining the support from over one-thirds of respondents

Number of ethics	Proportion of support	Actual contents
01	85.33%	Teachers have to perfect their qualities and set up a professional image.
15	79.90%	Teachers have to treat students fairly and equally.
07	76.62%	Teachers have to turn down inappropriate presents of all kinds so as not to damage their professional practices.
08	76.36%	Teachers have to avoid relationships which may involve the conflict of interests or the pursuance of personal interests.
14	74.07%	Teachers have to defend students' rights and interests and protect them from plausible damages.
04	73.87%	Teachers have to encourage students to explore and inquire.
21	71.97%	Teachers have to build up and develop a good relationship with students.
05	71.32%	Teachers have to improve their teaching methods, better their teaching contents, prepare for their teaching, and comply with the principles of education and professional ethics.
20	70.99%	Teachers have to respect the privacy of students and keep the personal data of students strictly confidential.
12	69.02%	Teachers have to pay attention to what they say and what they do so as to set up a role model for students.
02	68.89%	Teachers have to keep pace with the development of their knowledge fields and improve the quality of their teaching.

After rephrasing the selected professional ethics, the task force sent them to experts in linguistics for review and then incorporated the feedback from the experts so as to finalize the draft of the professional ethics for teachers in Macao for further consultation.

In September 2012 the task force printed another 5,000 promotional pamphlets incorporating a questionnaire on opinions about the draft of professional ethics for teachers in Macao: each respondent was asked whether they agreed on each of the eleven selected professional ethics. During this consultation period, in addition to distributing the pamphlets, the task force arranged for two mass meetings; there were about 150 number of attendance. In addition, in some social gatherings organized by the Chinese Educators Association of Macau where over 2,500 frontline teachers attended, the task force asked for 15 minutes to introduce to the teachers there about the progress of the task force. After a month's consultation, the task force collected 1,895 questionnaires and 1,818 were valid. Of the valid questionnaires, 89.36% agreed on the necessity for setting up professional ethics for teachers in Macao but 10.64% disagreed. Table 7.3 compares the responses from the two rounds of consultation.

Table 7.3. Responses to the two rounds of consultation

	First round of consultation (May and June 2012)	Second round of consultation (September 2012)
Questionnaires collected	1,527	1,895
Valid questionnaires	1,444	1,818
Proportion of those agreeing on the necessity for having professional ethics	87.63%	89.36%
Proportion of those disagreeing on the necessity for having professional ethics	12.37%	10.64%

While only about 10% of respondents disagreed on the necessity for having professional ethics, the reasons underlying their disagreements were analysed, as summarised in Table 7.4. Given that nearly about 90% of respondents are teachers, as indicated in the distribution of respondents displayed in Table 7.5, the results from the second round of consultation could be seen as representative of the views of frontline teachers in Macao.

In other words, the task force could somehow claim that there is a consensus among frontline teachers: for each of the 11 selected ethic, a significant majority of respondents – over 87% of respondents from the valid sample and over 98% of those who agree on the necessity for having professional ethics – agree that it is appropriate to include the ethics for Macao.

Table 7.4. Reasons for disagreeing on the necessity for having professional ethics found in the second round of consultation

Reason for disagreement	Proportion
It is counter-effective to have professional ethics.	18.75%
It is utterly unnecessary to have professional ethics.	50.96%
The task force cannot represent the views of teachers in Macao.	22.12%
Others	8.17%
Total	100.00%

Table 7.5. Distribution of the sample for the second round of consultation by the status of stakeholders in education

Stakeholder	Proportion in the sample
Teachers	87.28%
	(100.00%)
0-4 years of teaching experience	(20.11%)
5-9 years of teaching experience	(20.63%)
10-20 years of teaching experience	(32.87%)
21 years or above of teaching experience	(26.39%)
School administrators	7.08%
Staff at school	4.64%
Student teachers and others (including parents)	1.00%
Total	100.00%

After getting a consensus from frontline teachers, the task force continued its work on promoting the professional ethics in Macao. It was true that politics in the field of education was involved in setting up the professional ethics: each association in education wanted to claim credit for this task and did not want to work under the others. Yet, despite such political dynamics in the field of education, undeniably such collective effort of this task force on setting up professional ethics somehow suggests that many private school teachers are waking up to the need for the professionalism of teachers in Macao. This perhaps signals the beginning of the professional awakening of private school teachers in Macao.

CONCLUDING REMARKS

Before the passing of the Private Legal Frame, private school teachers in Macao, in stark contrast to their western counterparts, were not professionals on the one hand in that most of them were unqualified to teach, and they were not treated as professionals on the other in that their pay and benefits as well as their social status could be even worse than those of manual workers. This plight of private school teachers could be seen as a colonial legacy, resulting from the colonial neglect of education for the Chinese. Because of such neglect, basic education for the Chinese had been taken care of by the civic society. One important implication was a huge resource constraint in the provision of basic education; the quality of such kind of basic education was in serious doubt. Apart from that, such legacy also poses challenges to the professionalism of teachers in Macao and also obstacles to subsequent effort of enhancing the professionalism of teachers.

It is true that the Macao SAR government has been investing more and more resources in basic education, more specifically giving an increasing amount of subsidies to private schools; this could somehow play a role in enabling the professionalism of private school teachers. Yet, such increase in resource provision does not immediately make possible the professionalism of teachers. There has been resistance to such change; three sources of resistance could be identified. The first is from private schools. In the name of defending the autonomy of running a school in their own styles, private schools do not really make use of resources allocated by the Macao SAR government to improve the pay and benefits of their teachers. Instead, given their ultimate goal of survival, private schools seek to make use of resources allocated to boost up their reputation in order to enhance their student enrolment; to this end, private schools actually seek to exert a tight control over their teachers. Put simply, while allocating more and more resources to private schools in the hope that the quality of basic education could be improved, the Macao SAR government does not have effective mechanisms to ensure that private school teachers are treated by schools as professionals, let alone enhancing the professionalism of teachers.

The second source of resistance is from associations in the field of education in Macao. Given the colonial legacy, associations in the field of education have been formed by school principals and/or school administrators. It is true that associations in the field of education are meant to fight for improving the quality of education for the Chinese; but they are not meant to be a platform for teachers to voice out their needs and views. Rather, teachers have been marginalised and their voices have not been heard. While pledging to improve the quality of education, associations in the field of education do not mean to enhance the professionalism of teachers.

The third source of resistance is from private school teachers themselves. Because of the colonial legacy, there are quite a lot of unqualified teachers in the existing team of private school teachers in Macao. Given their background, it is not inconceivable that they are rather resistant to mechanisms towards professionalism, especially to mechanisms on reviewing their professional performances and assessing their professional growth, out of their fear and insecurity.

Despite the plight of private school teachers resulting from the colonial legacy, and despite resistance to effort of bringing in changes, the last decade has witnessed signs of the political and professional awakening of private school teachers. Perhaps it is still too early to pass judgement onto the professionalism of teachers in Macao. But the professionalism of teachers is well under way.

APPENDIX TABLES

Table A7.1. Members of Macao Chinese Educators Association in 2013

Position	Name (position at educational institution)
Chairperson	Chan, Hung (vice principal)
Vice chairperson	Wong, Kwok-Ying (principal); Cheng, Kit-Chiu (principal); Wong, Lai-Hing (principal); Ko, Kam-Fai (principal); Cheng, Kung-Kwong (principal); Au, Yu-Hung (principal); Sam, Yiu-Cheong (teacher)
General secretary	(also) Cheng, Hung-Kwong (principal)
Vice general secretary	Ng, Siu-Lan (head teacher)
Academic secretary	Chan, Chi-Fong (associate professor)
Academic vice secretary	Tang, Chun-Chit (associate professor); Ho Shing (principal)
Publication secretary	Yeung, Chai-Kei (principal)
Publication vice secretary	Lee, Ming-Kei (principal); Yeung, Pui-Yan (head teacher)
Organization secretary	Yeung, Kam-Tong (head teacher)
Organization vice secretary	Chan, Po-Sin (vice principal); Chan, Chun-Sun (head teacher)
Social secretary	Wong, Man-Sheung (teacher)
Social vice secretary	Ling, Wing-Sun (teacher); Siu, Fu-Pak (teacher)
Welfare secretary	Ip, Kai-Ching (head teacher)
Welfare vice secretary	Chan, Pik-Ling (teacher); Ho, Pui-Che (teacher)
Financial secretary	Kwok, King-Man (vice principal)
Financial vice secretary	Lee, Chau-Lam (vice principal)
Travel secretary	Hui, Shui-Kui (head teacher)
Travel vice secretary	Lee, Ying-Wei (head teacher); Lam, Wai-Lun (vice principal)

Table A7.2. Large-scale demonstrations in Macao, 2006-2011

Date of demonstration	Estimated number of participants (by the Police)	Estimated number of participants (by the organizer)	Major requests or slogans
2006/05/01	1,500	3,000	Kick out illegal labour; cut down labour from outside of Macao
2006/12/20	630	1,000	Kick out illegal labour; cut down labour from outside of Macao; lower the age for getting pension; free senior secondary education
2007/05/01	2,400	10,000	Against illegal labour and labour from outside of Macao; against the alliance of the government and merchants; against a high price of estate property; against corruption
2007/09/30	2,300	5,000	Insufficient parking places for motor-cycles
2007/10/01	1,300	5,000	Against corruption; secure livelihood; kick out labour from outside of Macao; insure local employment
2007/12/20	1,500	7,000	Against corruption; democracy; livelihood
2008/05/01	800	1,000	Cut down labour from outside of Macao; against illegal labour; more public housing; insure employment
2008/09/28	450	1,000	Fair and just recruitment mechanisms of civil servants
2008/10/01	120	300	Cut down labour from outside of Macao; against illegal labour; more public housing
2008/12/20	450	500	Against corruption; against labour from outside of Macao; against illegal labour; democracy
2009/05/01	400	500	Cut labour from outside of Macao; against illegal labour; improve livelihood; more public housing; no to merchants ruling Macao
2009/12/20	950	1,100	Against corruption; democracy; livelihood; getting over-age children from China to reunite with their parents

Date of demonstration	Estimated number of participants (by the Police)	Estimated number of participants (by the organizer)	Major requests or slogans
2010/05/01	1,500	---	Against labour from outside of Macao; against illegal labour; more public housing; enhance employment; care about the plight of the youth; resist against self-censorship
2010/10/01	80	150	Improve the health system; enhance property ownership; insure local employment; against inflation; stop the rise of the price of estate property; increase parking places for motor-cycles
2010/12/20	1,250	---	Against corruption; insure livelihood; democracy; stop the rise of the price of estate property; resist against self-censorship
2011/05/01	2,300	---	Against labour from outside of Macao; against illegal labour; more public housing; enhance employment; insure livelihood; getting over-age children from China to reunite with their parents; improve the situation of teachers; dissatisfaction with the routes of the light rail
2011/09/25	350	450	getting over-age children from China to reunite with their parents
2011/10/01	480	---	More public housing; enhance employment; stop the rise of the price of estate property; against inflation; getting over-age children from China to reunite with their parents; more transparency of the governance
2011/12/20	360	800	Against corruption; insure livelihood; democracy; getting over-age children from China to reunite with their parents

Source: Yu, 2010 quoted in an Appendix Table by Cheng and Wong, 2014.

Chapter 8

STUDENTS

It is self-evident that students are not merely users of an education system but products, so to speak, of a society – wherein the education system, together with the family and other social institutions such as the media, plays a significant role in shaping the characters of students. It is logical therefore to look at the student sector in order to understand the operation of the education system as a whole. As much as teachers and schools – and the colonial history of private schooling in Macao – have played their parts in establishing the quality of education, that quality is reflected to varying degrees in the performance of students.

It is common in many societies that youth is portrayed negatively. Social unrest among the young is often seen as overshadowing more serious and longstanding problems, even crime. So it is in Macao, where juvenile delinquency and so-called youth "sub-cultures" are seen as worrying. A lot attention is paid, for instance, to youth participation in apparent deviant acts such as physical assaults, drug dealing and addiction, internet addiction, gambling, and engaging in sexual 'trade', or escort activities (see the detailed yearly summaries of news for 1990-1999 in Chan, 2010). Following the strong economic development of Macao since 2004, and its increasing social affluence, the youth are now commonly condemned as too materialistic, overlooking the value of education. They are also criticized for being lazy and politically apathetic. As apparent proof of this, instead of engaging in academic work or meaningful social or cultural activities, many of the youth (including those studying at school) are spending a considerable amount of their time on part-time work (Wang et al., 2010). Some secondary-school students simply wait until they reach the legal working age to quit school and become a dealer in a casino: a high-paid job that does not require much formal education. Working part-time while at school or anticipating becoming a dealer at the age of eighteen, these students focus a lot on how much they can earn now in order so to spend on entertainment, fashion, accessories and expensive brands in particular, and to enjoy a luxurious life style in general. As a result, the youth are in general seen as short-sighted; not simply materialistic but as 'worshipping money.' These are all certainly interesting social phenomena, but these observations apply as much to adults in Macao. Two wrongs do not of course make a right, but our point is that the youth are scapegoated as either causing or particularly inhabiting such mind-set. Youth sub-cultures are beyond the scope of this book's investigative frame, but they can still be seen anecdotally as informing the education system. The focus of this chapter is therefore on two specific aspects of student life: academic performance and students' attitude towards schools and schooling.

We shall first discuss the academic performance of students in Macao, citing results reported for Macao in PISA 2009 (OECD, 2010) and a number of other educational indicators, in order to provide an overview of the general performance of students in education in Macao. We shall then move on to the attitude of students towards schools and schooling, referring again to related results reported for Macao in PISA 2009 (OECD, 2010). In addition to quantitative data, we shall draw on relevant qualitative data from the first author's projects: the views of students, expressed in individual in-depth interviews or in focus group interviews, towards the operation of schools, specifically their views on school regulations; and also an analysis of teaching practices in Macao. We point to the strict disciplining and enforced grade retention of students in Macao, and the role of students as effectively the sole source of guaranteed income for private schools, and suggest that these contribute to the disaffection of students in Macao.

ACADEMIC PERFORMANCE

A number of educational indicators allow us to gauge the overall academic of level of Macao students. Let us refer to them one by one. The first indicator is the Programme for International Student Assessment (PISA). This is not a curriculum-based assessment and does not strictly measure academic performance. However, it seeks to compare the comprehension, analytic ability and problem-solving skills of students across OECD countries and regions.

Table 8.1. The performance of 15-year-olds at PISA-Macao

Subject	PISA 2003		PISA 2006		PISA 2009	
	Average score of Macao	International average score	Average score of Macao	International average score	Average score of Macao	International average score
Reading	498	494	492	492	487	493
Mathematics	527	500	525	498	525	496
Science	525	500	511	500	511	501

Source: Chan, 2010: p. 232, Table 4.13.

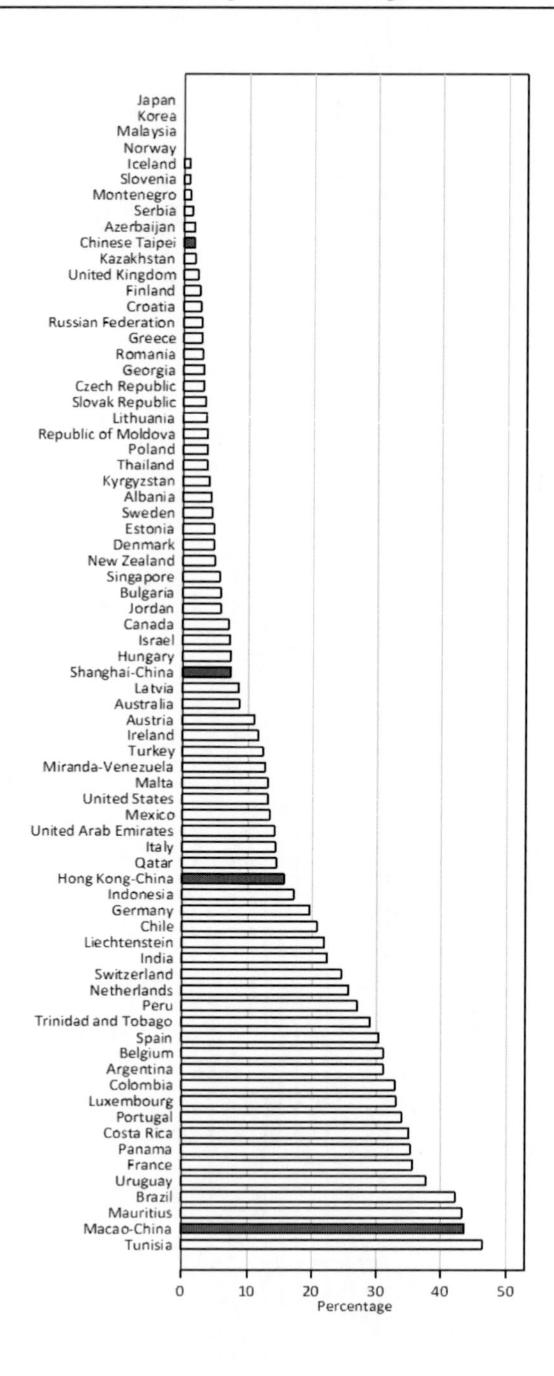

Figure 8.1. Accumulative rate of retention among PISA 2009 participants.

As a result of its practical basis, PISA also allows us to roughly deduce how well Macao students compare with others in reading, mathematics and science. As Table 8.1 indicates, the performance of Macao students has been about or above average among OECD participating countries and regions.

A further indicator is the number of students from Macao who proceed to university. It is commonly believed that 80% of students graduate to university. This compares favourably to the level in Hong Kong, another PRC administrative region, where the number has fluctuated between 16% and 18% since 1995. Many people in Macao are proud of this relative achievement. Critics point out that Macao has a less competitive and selective learning environment than Hong Kong, while others suggest that in contrast it is down to the strict grade retention many private schools employ.

An 80% graduation rate to university is, on the face of it, a significant achievement. However, this figure refers only to the proportion of students who graduate to university *directly* upon leaving secondary school – not all students of the relevant age. And this brings into question the practice of grade retention in Macao. As reported in PISA 2009 (OECD, 2010), the accumulated rate of grade retention in Macao is the second highest of all participating OECD countries and regions. As Figure 8.1 shows, some 40% of 15-year-olds have been retained at least once. Figure 8.2 shows further that 15% have been retained more than once:

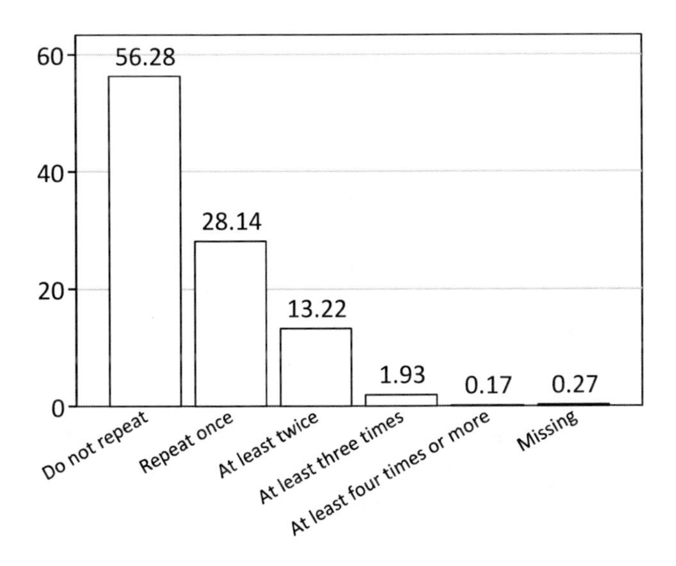

Figure 8.2. Proportion of students by number of grade retention in Macao.

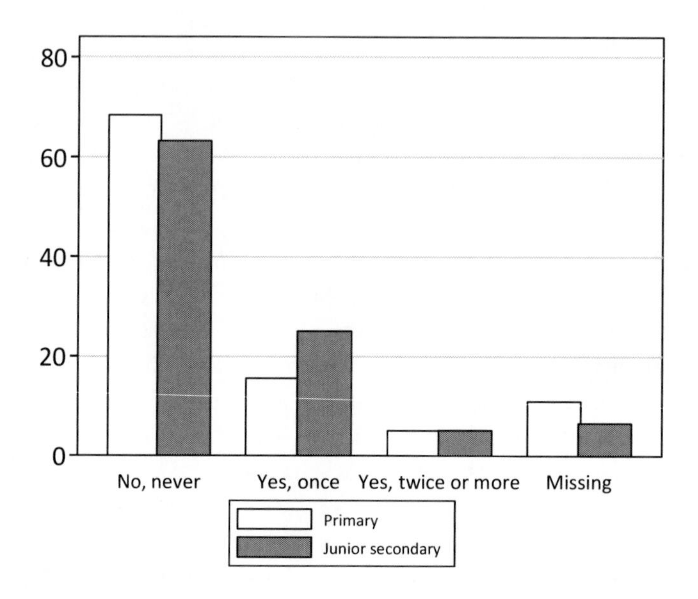

Figure 8.3. Proportion of students being retained at primary and junior secondary levels in Macao.

The cumulative effect of institutionalized grade retention throughout the system is alarming. According to one secondary school, when its senior secondary form-three students were asked about their experience of grade retention, 76% said they had been retained. It might be reasonable to infer from this that only a minority of students in Macao complete their education without being retained. Indeed, the rates of retention at different educational levels have remained high since the 1999 handover. Table 8.2 tracks those rates over time: the rate has been over 5% at primary level, on average about 15% at junior secondary level, and above 6% at senior secondary level.

Grade retention is found to be a significant predictor of school dropout in the West (e.g., Jimerson et al., 2002; Ream and Rumberger, 2008; Roderick, 1994; Roderick and Nagaoka, 2005). It would not be unreasonable to assume that this is also the case in Macao. Even without standardized testing in Macao, schools have found in grade retention a different way to screen off students before the end of their secondary education.

The most up to date figures on school drop-out rates (featured on the Macao DSEJ website) are rather uninformative. In order to strengthen them, we have examined students' *completion* rate. Table 8.3 shows the completion rate of students at every level improving gradually since 1999. However, at no point does the completion rate at any stage top 80%.

Table 8.2. Grade retention rates in Macao, 1999-2010 (%)

Academic year	1999/ 2000	2000/ 2001	2001/ 2002	2002/ 2003	2003/ 2004	2004/ 2005	2005/ 2006	2006/ 2007	2007/ 2008	2008/ 2009	2009/ 2010
Primary level	7.3	6.9	7.0	5.9	5.7	5.5	5.5	5.6	5.9	5.2	5.2
Junior secondary level	15.6	16.3	16.7	15.7	14.7	14.9	15.3	15.6	15.4	13.9	13.8
Senior secondary level	7.6	8.2	8.1	7.4	5.9	6.5	7.0	7.3	7.1	6.6	5.9

Source: Chan , 2010:p.230, Table 4.10.

Table 8.3. The completion rate of Macao, 1999-2010

Educational Stage	1999/ 2000	2000/ 2001	2001/ 2002	2002/ 2003	2003/ 2004	2004/ 2005	2005/ 2006	2006/ 2007	2007/ 2008	2008/ 2009	2009/ 2010
Pre-primary	92.0	93.5	93.5	94.2	94.5	94.4	94.8	93.6	94.3	93.3	94.6
Primary	78.5	81.4	82.7	83.2	83.1	84.1	84.6	84.0	84.4	86.0	85.7
Secondary	58.8	61.9	62.5	65.0	68.5	66.0	67.4	66.6	66.3	65.9	63.8
Junior secondary	68.5	66.6	67.4	69.8	70.7	70.7	68.1	68.8	70.7	72.7	72.9
Senior secondary	65.9	70.3	70.5	73.7	77.3	74.1	74.8	76.1	76.8	77.0	78.1

Source: Chan , 2010.

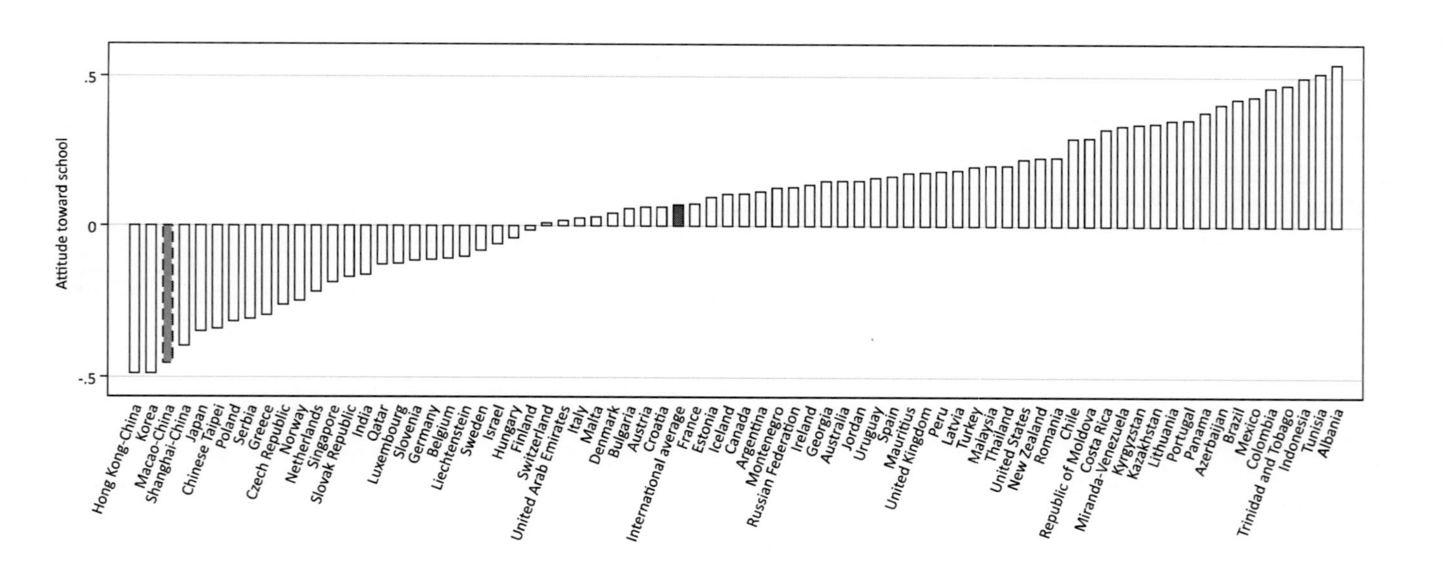

Figure 8.4. PISA findings – attitude towards schools compared with OECD/international average.

This means that at least 20% of students never complete secondary education. This could be described as the drop-out rate, and it is an alarmingly high figure. Furthermore, despite all the changes and investment to education since 1999, student completion rate has barely improved.

In view of these indicators, we would comment that the performance of Macao students does not appear particularly extraordinary. Despite the apparent 80% graduation rate to university, the performance of Macao's students compared to their PISA peers is just about average. This is doubly concerning in light of the increased amount of centralized spending on education since 1999: between 5% and 15% of students are retained at each grade, especially at junior secondary level. The idea that at least 20% of students fail to complete basic education leads us to consider the effects of the schooling environment on students.

Attitude towards Schools and Schooling

In addition to general aptitude testing, PISA also asks questions about students' attitudes towards schools and schooling. Macao students generally score high in disaffection and low in a sense of belonging to schools (OECD, 2004, 2007, 2010). Figure 8.4 displays the result for PISA 2009. We argue that such results are closely related to the schooling environment in Macao.

Quantitative indicators do not explain this disaffection and lack of sense of belonging. This brings us to qualitative data obtained from research, and to some anecdotal observations from the first author. The qualitative data is presented tentatively, and has not been sufficiently tested in terms of its statistical representativeness, yet we believe that it still offers insights into the general schooling environment in Macao. This environment is dominated by three main features: curriculum, pedagogy, and assessment. Let us treat them one by one:

School Regulations

As discussed in Chapter 6, private schools receive government money in line with the number of students they recruit to every grade and level. At the same time, private schools have complete legal autonomy in how they treat and assess students. With no standardized examinations in Macao, there is no objective way for students or their parents to assess the effectiveness and success of an individual school, so schools place great emphasis on the conduct and discipline of their students. Our focus here is therefore on students' general perception of school regulations and how they are enforced.

It would take another book to analyse the reasonableness of school regulations in Macao, so let us assume that some basic rationales are followed. These rationales have to do with the stated ethos of the school itself, if not with any identified educational philosophy. Even where educational missions differ between schools, it is possible to identify trends among the schools as a whole, and to discuss them in terms of how reasonable and unreasonable they are. As an example, an elite school sets out the following two regulations: first, all students have to obey teachers' commands at all times in all places; second, no students should challenge the previous regulation. What many students find objectionable is that school regulations of such kind command students' unquestionable obedience. As is seen in Chapter 7, many teachers in focus group interviews accept the necessity of strict regulation of students without question. Such teachers' responses are quoted below:

> 'Of course, we need school regulations. (…) Just like there are laws in society, so there are school regulations in schools. Without them, society would become chaotic; likewise, schools would become uncontrollable.' (A teacher, in a focus group interview conducted by the first author)

> 'Yes, some regulations are rather tedious or outdated; some simply don't make sense. (…) And in some cases, it's rather difficult to enforce. For example, how could schools expect us to be able to see by the naked eye the length of students' socks, especially when boys are wearing long trousers? (…) But, I still think it's necessary to have school regulations. Otherwise, how could students be kept under control? (…) Without something in black and white, it's difficult to explain to students why they are being punished.' (A teacher, in a focus group interview conducted by the first author)

> 'I think, each school is entitled to have its own school regulations to keep their students in order. (…) So I don't see the point of discussing whether school regulations are controversial or unreasonable. That's irrelevant. (…) It's a bit like commenting on the decoration of a person's apartment; it's none of people's business how a person's apartment is decorated. (…) Even if a school sets up some so-called controversial or unreasonable regulations, it's none of their business. (…) If students

don't like the regulations, they can go to a school with regulations they like. It's up to them; they could leave and choose to study in somewhere else.' (A teacher, in a focus group interview conducted by the first author)

In an environment where teachers accept regulation in general as a matter of fact, it is perhaps unsurprising that they are disinclined to express opinions on individual regulations that may negatively impact on their students. A number of teachers did identify unreasonable regulations, however, as did nearly all of the students polled for this book. Here are some examples:

> 'I think it's unreasonable to impose very strictly a particular shoe style on all students. (...) Many school regulations related to appearance are unreasonable. Basically, with such school uniforms, schools simply want students to look stupid.' (A student, in a focus group interview conducted by the first author)

> 'It doesn't make sense to make so many specific requirements about our school uniforms, e.g., the length of our socks and trousers and skirts, the colour of our shoes (what kind of black) and sneakers (what kind of white), the design of our shoes, and even the colour of our bras and underwear. It is rather ridiculous. (...) And it's a waste of time to make sure that students' hair is so-called "naturally" black.' (A student, in a focus group interview conducted by the first author)

> 'I don't think it makes much sense to give students a demerit whenever they are late. Three demerits make one big demerit; and three big demerits lead to disqualification. That means, when students are late nine times, they will be kicked out of school. A student can get kicked out of school for being late nine times in all their school years!' (A student, in a focus group interview conducted by the first author)

Students in general find regulations about their appearance and behaviour rather annoying. If these regulations merely appeared on paper, they would not have much impact. But they are in fact rigorously enforced every day. Given the low status of teachers in schools and in society, there is little to profit a teacher into standing up to management on behalf of students. What particularly annoys students is inconsistency in applying these regulations. According to our research, there are two main reasons for these inconsistencies; they are different but related. First, teachers may simply interpret regulations differently to other teachers; secondly, they may interpret them very differently depending on the individual student. Nearly all students interviewed for this book made similar points:

> 'Teachers are very subjective in interpreting school regulations. (...) For example, it is written that all students should wear white sneakers. (...) But the judgements of the whiteness of sneakers are not consistent between different teachers. (...) I remember a classmate's sneakers were getting old and they looked like yellow; and a teacher forced him to buy a new pair of sneakers immediately, simply because the teacher considered the colour of sneakers to be yellow or not white enough. (...) But, other teachers didn't enforce the same school regulation.' (A student, in focus group interview conducted by the first author)

> 'You know, hair would turn brown when you use hair-dryer every day. (...) My form teacher insisted that I violated a school regulation in that I dyed my hair into gold but actually it wasn't true. (...) Even when I explained to her why my hair looked gold, but was actually brown, the teacher still insisted that I had to have my hair cut.' (A student, in a focus group interview conducted by the first author)

> 'Well, I think many teachers are partial. If they like you, you won't have any problems even if you obviously violate a school regulation. (...) But, teachers would find a way to accuse you of violating school regulations even when you don't. (...) It's very important to please teachers so as to avoid problems.' (A student, in a focus group interview conducted by the first author)

What students found particularly unacceptable was that teachers were both judges and executors of school regulations, and that there were no mechanisms for appeal when students disagreed with teachers' judgments. When some students were courageous enough to voice out about their teachers' misjudgements or maltreatments, the students would usually be punished for being disrespectful. The following example articulated in a lecture of the first author's is also commonly heard in many focus group interviews with students, as well as in individual interviews with evening-school students:

> 'A classmate of mine has his hair touch his collar. A teacher said that he had to have it cut; otherwise, he would be given a demerit for violating a school regulation on required hair length. The following day, that classmate came to school with a skin-head and did not violate any school

regulations; but he was still punished. The teacher said that the classmate was challenging his authority by such rebellious behaviour.' (A student, in class discussion in one lecture conducted by the first author)

Table 8.4. Responses to questions on teachers: 'How much do you disagree or agree with each of the following statements about teachers at your school?' PISA 2009 – A comparison of Macao and OECD average

Question	Response	Macao (%)	OECD Average (%)
I get along well with most teachers.	Strongly disagree	2.45	3.71
	Disagree	14.11	11.49
	Agree	69.43	59.55
	Strongly agree	13.78	24.38
	Missing	0.22	0.87
Most teachers are interested in my well-being.	Strongly disagree	4.28	6.83
	Disagree	31.61	26.30
	Agree	56.46	54.12
	Strongly agree	7.34	11.49
	Missing	0.30	1.27
Most of my teachers really listen to what I have to say.	Strongly disagree	7.93	6.20
	Disagree	38.39	26.28
	Agree	48.21	55.51
	Strongly agree	4.96	10.79
	Missing	0.52	1.22
Most of my teachers treat me fairly.	Strongly disagree	7.58	5.12
	Disagree	21.48	15.87
	Agree	61.74	61.35
	Strongly agree	8.85	16.39
	Missing	0.36	1.27

Put simply, students are expected to be compliant and obedient. There is no room for students to voice different opinions, including their understandings of school regulations and their views on teachers' interpretations, let alone to pose challenges to teachers. As we have seen, few teachers question either the practice or reasonableness of school regulations. For this reason, it is nigh-on inconceivable that a teacher would openly sympathize with a student, let alone take a student's side in a dispute about overall regulations.

No wonder, then, that Macao students get on poorly with their teachers as compared with other OECD countries, as is indicated in Table 8.4. And no wonder either that the students' attitude towards teachers comes to influence how teachers treat them. Students report that the focus of many teachers is simply on making a class absolutely quiet, and thereby disciplined. Perhaps this explains the figures for class control attested to in Table 8.5.

Table 8.5. Responses to questions on lessons: 'How often do these things happen in your [test language] lessons?' PISA 2009 – A comparison of Macao and OECD average

Question	Response	Macao (%)	OECD Average (%)
There is noise and disorder.	Never or hardly ever	24.23	20.48
	Some lessons	61.09	47.25
	Most lessons	11.66	22.23
	All lessons	2.53	8.97
	Missing	0.49	1.06
The teacher has to wait a long time for students to quieten down.	Never or hardly ever	26.93	28.53
	Some lessons	56.34	42.58
	Most lessons	13.01	19.68
	All lessons	3.2	8.02
	Missing	0.52	1.19
Students do not start working for a long time after the lesson begins.	Never or hardly ever	23.51	32.53
	Some lessons	55.61	41.38
	Most lessons	16.12	17.62
	All lessons	4.24	7.52
	Missing	0.52	1.13

Put simply, students are expected to keep quiet, remain obedient, and sit still at all times; meanwhile, teachers are doing their best to monitor students very closely to keep them always under absolute control. In other words, the schooling environment in Macao in general is rather coercive. Given such an atmosphere, it is unsurprising that some students even compare schools to prisons, as quoted below.

> 'Teachers are just making a living out of their job; you can't expect them to give you special treatment just because you need extra help. (…) "Normal" people don't like schools. (…) Schools are "prisons." (…) Staying in such a boring place for so long is not much different from staying in prison. (…) But we have no choice; you have to go to "prison" in exchange for a diploma. (...) I just hate school.' (An evening-school student, in an individual interview with the first author)

The Teaching Setup: Curriculum, Pedagogy, and Assessment

Apart from school regulations, the teaching setup of Macao – including curriculum, pedagogy, and assessment – also provides an important key to understanding the schooling environment in Macao. Some teaching and administrative arrangements are perhaps unique to Macao. Before we move on to discuss curriculum, pedagogy and assessment in Macao schools, let us first turn to these very specific arrangements.

In Macao, every subject at a particular grade is usually taught by the same teacher. That is to say, for each subject, only one teacher is responsible for deciding what to teach, allocating time to different topics, arranging a variety of home assignments throughout the year, designing the format and contents of tests and examinations, and also choosing a passing standard. The teacher will have to submit an annual plan to the school, and will be visited in class by the principal or senior administrators two or three times a year, but apart from this there are no formal mechanisms by which schools can monitor and assess the professional performance of teachers. The practice is therefore largely to leave teachers alone, except in cases of grave seriousness. There is therefore no guarantee that Macao teachers' teaching is up to a professional standard.

In order not to cause any trouble, so to speak, teachers in Macao can easily adjust the level of difficulty for tests and examinations so that they could meet the passing rate and eventually the rate of grade retention set by the school. In fact, it is not unheard of for some teachers to design an extremely easy test paper so that all students could pass so as to avoid potential criticisms by their schools. Nor is it unheard of that that some teachers in elite schools make a test extremely difficult so that very few students can pass, thereby establishing the teacher's reputation. Despite this variation, the underlying theme is the same: teachers set the academic standard, and with no effective monitoring, they are free to manipulate student results to suit either personal or business agendas. As such, where students underperform, there is no way of telling where the problem begins and ends. Is it the student or is it the teaching? This is reinforced by a culture in which the teacher is unchallengeable in the classroom. A coercive learning environment and opaque grading has very often been a perfect recipe for high grade retention.

Administrative arrangements within schools are a further reinforcing factor. Teachers are obliged to submit students' grades to the administrative faculty at the end of each semester, in order that report cards may be prepared. Even in cases where a student or a teacher discovers a mistake in grading, this mistake can very often not be corrected, because the report card is already in production. A set working schedule is therefore prioritised over student achievement. This is not only unfair, but reinforces the imbalance of power between students and teachers.

Some of these problems are undoubtedly down to the relative youth of Macao's education system. Once an entirely voluntary enterprise, it only developed its first tertiary institutions in the 1980s. Macao's schools, therefore, were aimed at preparing students for universities abroad: mainly in Hong Kong, Taiwan and the PRC. As a result, multiple curriculums co-existed. The problems with this can be illustrated by a single academic example: that of Geography. Depending on the curriculum a student was studying, they would learn a great deal about the landscape of Hong Kong, or Taiwan, or China, but they would learn almost nothing about Macao. While curriculums in many countries are often criticized for being unrelated to real life, this tendency was particular marked – and even surreal – in Macao. This perhaps helps to explain the high level of student disaffection in Macao compared to that reported by other OECD countries and regions.

Teachers in Macao sometimes have to teach a number of curriculums at once, in order to prepare students for different entrance examinations outside of Macao. This led to a very tight teaching schedule and an extremely didactic mode of teaching. Put simply: teachers talked and students listened. Complicating this was the issue of class size in private schools. In 1999, a class could have 50 or 60 students; it still averages 35. One can well argue that interactive teaching is simply not possible in such an environment. Even if it were, however, the culture of teaching in Macao is such that interaction is not encouraged. Classroom discipline is very often held to be the ultimate goal. Given the tight schedules for each curriculum, teachers are obliged to stuff their students with information rather than actually teach them. Student-centred learning is a cliché in many countries, so it remains alarming that the classroom in Macao is so teacher-dominated. Many students report that boring classes are the norm:

> 'Classes are so boring. (…) Teachers talk endlessly and pointlessly. (…) Usually I would sleep in classes and teachers don't mind so much about it. As long as you remain quiet so that they could keep talking, teachers don't care what you do in classes. (…) The point is not to disturb them. (…) I don't see the point of going to school – what can you learn from teachers teaching like that? (…) Teachers actually don't care about whether we students understand what they teach them, they just finish

what they have planned to teach.' (A student, in discussion in one lecture conducted by the first author)

Didactic teaching is explicitly and implicitly examination-oriented. Many examinations are simple tests of a student's fact-recognition capabilities. The ability to memorize a fact is taken, perhaps not unreasonably, as a measure of how well as student has understood it. But if 90% or 100% of questions in a test are about previously memorized facts, simple understanding is being privileged over engagement. As one teacher puts it (already quoted in Chapter 6):

> 'I was a new teacher teaching the Chinese language in that school (...) I was shocked to learn that in a test all questions are fill-in-the-banks asking students about facts of what we had taught. (...) So, I suggested to my colleagues that perhaps we could have at least one open-ended question – 10 marks out of 100– requiring students to come up with their own answers. (...) But my colleagues refused and said that it would be difficult to come up with a standardized way to grade an open-ended question. (...) I feel rather frustrated with such an attitude.' (A teacher, personal communication with the first author)

An experienced retired teacher reinforces the point (also quoted in Chapter 6):

> 'I had been teaching Geography for years – and I had taught curriculums set by Taiwan, the PRC, and Hong Kong. (...) When I went through examination scripts set by the Hong Kong Examinations Authority and compared them with scripts set by teachers in Macao, I realised that what was tested in Hong Kong students and in Macao students was rather different. (...) Give you an example. In our examinations, Macao students were asked questions like "What is the height of the Mount Himalaya?". But, in Hong Kong examinations, I found that students would first be asked some facts, such as what different symbols represented in a map. Then they would be asked to decide if they were going to set up a wood-producing factory, where they would set it and why they would decide to do it that way. You see, Hong Kong students are expected not only to recall some factual information, but also to understand the given situation and to analyse it. (...) Put simply, from the ways in which assessments are set, we can see that Macao students are just expected to memorize loads of facts but are not

trained to be analytical.' (A retired teacher, in an interview from a series of interviews conducted by the authors)

Curriculum, pedagogy, and assessment are three inter-dependent and inter-related areas of teaching; each influences how the other two operate. In Macao, the curriculums are about a huge amount of content irrelevant to students' lives. What is assessed is about recognizing a huge amount of irrelevant factual information. Given that such an amount of facts has to be taught within a short period of time, it is taught didactically. Taking curriculum, pedagogy, and assessment altogether, we can see that students in Macao are forced to learn foreign curriculums or something irrelevant to their real life, to learn in a passive, if not alienated, way, and to be assessed one-dimensionally. Their grades in school are therefore open to teachers' manipulation. This helps explain why so many students find schooling a waste of time, if not suffocating, and why disaffection among Macao students ranks so high among OECD countries and regions.

Concluding Remarks

The Macao SAR government has steadily increased its investment in education since 1999. The pace of investment has quickened in line with the post-2004 economic boom. However, the academic performance of students does not appear to have increased in line with investment. In fact, looking at the PISA comparisons, it might even be said to be deteriorating. This is especially alarming given the low completion rate of basic education among Macao students.

Surely, we could say that social factors outside schooling play a part in explaining the low completion rate. If students can make good money working as a cashier in a casino for instance, the link between education and employment is fundamentally weakened. This has led to accusations that young people in Macao overlook the instrumental importance of education. There is some truth in this interpretation, and a general anti-intellectual bent in Macao society to reinforce it. But this interpretation overlooks the schooling environment. In the foregoing, we have demonstrated how school regulations and the teaching set-up in private schools contribute to a coercive schooling environment. This environment serves to alienate students, which leads to underperformance. Such underperformance is not, therefore, a matter of an individual student's failure, but a social problem resulting from in-built structural deficits in the education system as a whole.

Chapter 9

CONCLUSION

We began this book by highlighting a number of issues about the quality of education in Macao that the public consider alarming. We focused on the high rate of grade retention, a low completion rate of basic education (an elevated drop-out rate before completing high-school), and a high level of student disaffection with schooling.

We also discussed the boom of the gambling – or gaming – industry since 2004. This has led to an abundance of jobs in Macao, particularly for the young, and a broader increase in GDP and the general affluence of citizens of Macao. The average casino dealer earns more than the average schoolteacher. Where educational failures have occurred, the trend in both the press and the civic society has been to put most of the blame on individual students, seeing them as short-sighted youths who overlook the instrumental importance of education in favour of materialistic desires. This means that when discussing general trends in education, such as the high rate of grade retention and the low incidence of completing basic education, individualistic explanations have been preferred.

A student's failure in education is generally put down to their desire for immediate material gain: they prefer to work in a casino (for a high wage with little chance of promotion) rather than put themselves on a clear professional path. And perhaps there is some truth in this. However, in focusing on individualistic explanations, Macao's civil society glosses over the in-built structural or institutional factors that impact on the education system; and, some of which date from the colonial era. This book has sought to correct for this oversight by examining the operations of schools and the practices of frontline teachers in Macao.

In our conclusion, we shall first summarize our analysis of the demonstrably poor quality of basic education in Macao, highlighting what needs to be addressed if the situation is to change. Secondly, we shall report on what has already been done to effect change and underscore the major obstacles to bringing change about. Finally, we shall discuss what can be learnt from the case of Macao concerning the recent international advocacy of the privatization of education.

THE IMPACT OF THE COLONIAL LEGACY FOR EDUCATION IN MACAO

In order to understand the existing Macao education system, it is absolutely necessary to look at the history of Macao. Under colonial Portuguese rule, education for the local Chinese was ignored by the government and shouldered by civil organizations, including religious organizations (mainly the Catholic Church).

This meant that effectively all education for the Chinese population was undertaken by private schools. For a long time, these schools had no recourse to government funds, which meant that there was no coordinated curriculum or standardized testing. Consequently, while there were a growing number of schools, there could not really be said to be an educational infrastructure in Macao.

The results of this governmental neglect were obvious, and still have not been entirely rectified. Without government support, private schools in Macao could rarely afford to hire qualified teachers. Indeed, given the autonomy born of neglect, schools could hire anyone they liked.

Things might have been different if the colonial government had provided basic teacher training, but its focus was very much on instructing Portuguese children. But as things stood, anybody could become a teacher in a private school as long as the school principal liked them.

As a result, teaching has never been quite treated as a legitimate profession in Macao, and teachers have not been treated as professionals. This trend has become to a large extent a self-fulfilling prophecy: if teachers are not considered as professionals, then the professionalism of teachers will not be considered a priority. Combined with a weak educational infrastructure throughout Macao, the overall quality of education remains in serious doubt.

What Has Been Done to Change the Situation and What Are the Obstacles to Reform?

Macao is a post-colonial society, but the legacy of colonialism (and particularly the neglect of the native Chinese population by the Portuguese colonial government) has had effects that persist to the present day. The chaotic educational infrastructure and the lack of universal qualifications for teachers are very much a part of this legacy. The post-colonial SAR government has invested an abundance of resources to tackle both of these problems. Indeed, as Table A9.1 shows, education in Macao has broadly improved. The SAR government has put an especial effort into centralizing the organization of education throughout Macao – stressing the necessities of free and compulsory education for people up to the age of 21, increased support for funding and training of teachers, and an equitable pay and benefits package for teachers.

However, these government initiatives have met with resistance both from private schools and from individual teachers. The key to this argument is that while private schools were under-funded during colonial rule, they also had more or less complete legal autonomy: they could set their own curriculums, they could decide on their own term times, they could design (and audit) their own exams; they could hire and fire teachers on a whim; and they could exclude students without having to explain themselves. Macao's Basic Law guarantees private schools these rights to this day. This means that while the SAR government has a legal responsibility to improve education, every effort at standardization has been resisted by private schools.

The exception to this rule has been the extension of basic education to cover fifteen years, with three years of pre-school, six years of primary school and six years of secondary school being guaranteed (free to parents) from 2006. But there has been no equivalent extension of standards to the design of curriculums and examinations. The result is that schools in Macao generally teach a curriculum imported from elsewhere: from China, from Taiwan, from Hong Kong, or a mixture of all three – with no standardized examination to decide who has graduated or not.

Basic education has spread across Macao, and has become increasingly better resourced, which has effectively meant that the entire system has become government funded. Private schools, previously excluded from government funds, are now in receipt of a large amount of government money – without necessarily having to change their focus in accordance to government diktat. Crucially, this means that when private schools compete for students they are also competing for the per-student subsidy that comes from the government. This has created a kind of educational arms race. To get new students, private schools have to demonstrate not only their overall academic standards but their broader social and economic desirability. Hence the reluctance of such schools to submit to standardized curriculums and assessment: standardized testing may actually harm the schools' social standing. The bulk of this resistance comes from well-known or otherwise high-ranking schools in Macao, which would not like to be returned to a level playing-field with other, less acclaimed schools. The result is that an individual school's grade retention levels or disciplinary regulations cannot be accurately gauged against those of another school. This partly explains the high rate of grade retention in Macao (in that grade retention holds up student numbers, regardless of the performance of individual students). Research in the USA has suggested a close link between grade retention and school drop-out – meaning that students who are retained tend to exit schooling earlier than students who progress.

The result in Macao is that private schools tend to place a greater emphasis on keeping students under control, rather than inspiring them to excel academically. And this in turn means tight control of teachers. Indeed, there are many parallels between the way students and teachers are treated by their schools. School regulations seek to mold the appearance and conduct of students; teacher manuals seek to do the same for teachers. This is one reason that the "professionalization" of teachers works against the immediate interests of schools in Macao: if you professionalize teachers; you empower them to be themselves.

Despite this, teachers in Macao have recently gone through a professional awakening. With greater government funding to schooling, teachers have begun to question why they are seeing little in the way of progress with regard to pay and job security. Schools in Macao are generally moving towards employing teachers with a diploma in education, if not a university degree, and the number of qualified teachers in Macao is growing all the time. However, private schools still educate 95% of the school-age population, and these schools are under no legal obligation to hire qualified staff. Indeed, hiring a few well qualified teachers can work to maintain a school's reputation while doing nothing to improve its educational achievements. Despite improved terms for teachers across Macao, the work of teaching is still not seen as "professional". Even fully qualified teachers may find that Macao's gambling industry provides better job options. So while teachers in Macao have become better qualified since 1999, it remains to be seen if the quality of education they provide is probably better.

To sum up, the infrastructure of education in Macao has been much improved since 1999. Private schools remain resistant to centralized assessment, either of students or of teachers, which means that the professionalism and achievements of teachers is still very much in doubt. In this book, we have argued that the combination of unaccountable private schools and untested teachers makes for a very dubious education system; indeed, one that is providing a poor education in general.

Lessons Learned from the Case of Macao

Macao's education system has certain unique aspects, but it still provides an ideal test case for an examination of the neoliberal discourse currently dominant in education across the developed world. This neoliberal system can be defined by the belief that a national (or otherwise government-controlled) schooling system is inefficient and ineffective and should be replaced with a cost-effective privatized school system. The keywords for neoliberalism in education are: market, competition, parental choice and quality of education.

Under an idealized national schooling system, the practices of all schools are governed by the state and thus standardized. In the neoliberal reading, all schools in such a system would basically be the same, implying little choice for parents and their children. Crucially, without competition, the quality of teaching of schools would not measurably improve. In such a uniform system, schools would be neither efficient nor effective. By contrast, the neoliberal doctrine would have it that if schools were removed from state governance and standardized testing, there would be much more room for innovation, individuality and the materialization of different educational missions. In this world, schools with different styles and missions would compete in an open market for students based on the different needs and goals of those students and society in general.

This view holds that students (and their parents) will ultimately and rationally decide on the school that fits them best. Furthermore, in the neoliberal view, competition is believed to boost the overall quality of education: good schools would win students; poor schools would not. In the long run, society would benefit from such competition introduced at such an early stage in students' life. However, the case of Macao urges us to rethink the potential benefits of a privatized schooling system where education is seen as a market and students and their parents viewed as customers. Contrary to what neoliberal discourse would have us believe, in order to increase their market visibility and reputation to attract more students, schools and teachers do not necessarily make an effort to be more pedagogically innovative or to develop their niches to meet different needs of students. Rather, different schools and their teachers could and would resort to manipulations of various kinds wherever and whenever necessary to promote students' academic achievements and to boost their academic reputation so as to make them look attractive to students and their parents. It goes without saying that such manipulations and related practices are not necessarily beneficial to individual students or conducive to improving the overall quality of education. When all schools are doing similar things to promote students' academic achievements to boost up their academic reputation, there is actually little to choose between schools beyond their anecdotal reputation. Similarly, if all schools are engaged in a kind of subterfuge to keep enrolment numbers high, it is difficult for parents to make an informed choice about which school is best. The example of Macao suggested that privatized schooling can actually be damaging, and that such competitive (and sometimes deceptive) practices ultimately cause damage to students.

In saying this, we do not mean to assert that a privatized schooling system is wrong by definition or to defend a nationalized schooling system as ideal. Rather, our point is that letting the practices of schools be regulated by "the market", and thereby emphasizing competition between institutions, does not necessarily give customers more choices or guarantee efficiency and effectiveness in the provision of education, let alone the provision of *quality* education.

APPENDIX

Table A9.1. Chronology of major incidents impacting on the development of education in Macao

Year	Incident
1966 15th November	The conflict between the Portuguese government and the local Chinese over the construction of a school (坊眾學校) in Taipa triggered the '12.3' incident.
1966 3rd December	The '12.3' incident
1977 22nd October	The first law concerning the provision of subsidies from the colonial government to private schools was passed.

Year	Incident
1978	The colonial government compiled a list of 48 non-profit-making private schools that could receive subsidies from the government.
1981	The Chinese Educators Association of Macao sent separate requests to the government and the Legislative Council asking for an increase in the amount of subsidies to private schools and a tax exemption of private school teachers.
1981	The Macao Catholic Schools Association was established.
1985	A teacher training course jointly offered by the South China Normal University, the DSEJ, and the Chinese Educators Association of Macao became available.
1985	The Chinese Educators Association of Macao sent a request to the colonial government asking for the implementation of nine-year compulsory education.
1986	The Chinese Educators Association of Macao was commissioned by the government to get students without proper documents registered.
1988	The Macao Governor announced that the government planned to promote the Portuguese language before the handover of Macao to the PRC.
1989	The colonial government allocated subsidies to students enrolling in non-profit making private schools; the amount was MOP 500 a year.
1990	While the law 11/91/M was in the making, the public hotly debated over whether the Portuguese language should be a second language of instruction.
1991	The law 11/91/M was announced.
1991	Given a shortage of finances, the colonial government put the implementation of free primary education on hold.
1992	The colonial government reset an education committee, an official consultative committee working directly under the Macao Governor.
1993	The school net was implemented; the number of schools constructed was on proportion to the size of population in each district and the DSEJ funded part of the construction fees.
1993	A decree on the constitution of private educational institutions was announced.
1994	A decree on the pre-primary, primary, and secondary education programmes was announced.
1995	The decree on adult education was announced.
1995	The provision of education for all was implemented; and the colonial government intended to provide it for free. 39 private schools joined the public school net (free education school connection) and 25,000 students, about half the student population in Macao at the time, benefited from this.
1996	A decree on the regulation of teaching staff hired by private schools was announced.
1996	The second phase of the expansion of public school net was kicked started.
1997	The second phase of the provision of free basic education was started; free education would be extended to junior secondary education in the academic year of 1998.
2000	The Macao SAR government announced the promotion of IT education policy.
2002	In view of a decrease in student population, the Macao SAR government promoted creative education so as to facilitate the implementation of small class teaching.
2003	The Macao SAR government started a consultation on the review of the educational policy.
2003	Private school teachers were required to pay income tax.
2004	In reviewing the educational policy, the public was debating whether free education should be extended to pre-primary education or to senior secondary education.

Table A9.1. (Continued)

Year	Incident
2006	The law 9/2006 was announced.
2007	The DSEJ started to promote school-based comprehensive evaluation.
2007	It was announced that fifteen-year free education would be promoted in the academic year of 2007/2008.
2007 1st October	About 100 teachers took to the streets to express their concern over educational issues and raise concern about the issue of teachers' pressure.
2008	The Macao SAR government started consultative work over the establishment of 'the Private Legal Frame'.
2011 1st May	About 800 teachers took to the streets asking for the establishment of 'the Private Legal Frame'.
2011	'The Private Legal Frame' was officially discussed in the Legislative Council.
2012 March	'The Private Legal Frame' was passed.

APPENDICES

APPENDIX A.
A LIST OF SECONDARY SCHOOLS IN MACAO BY SCHOOL TYPE

I. SCHOOLS ORGANIZED BY TRADITIONAL ORGANIZATIONS

1. Escola Tong Sin Tong (同善堂中學)
2. Escola Tong Nam (Tong Nam School/東南學校)
3. Escola Secundaria Pui Va (Pui Va Middle School/培華中學)
4. Escola Pui Tou (Pooi To Middle School/培道中學)
5. Escola Kao Yip (Kao Yip Middle School/教業中學)
6. Escola para Filhos e Irmãos dos Operários (Secundário) (The Workers' Children High School, Macau/勞工子弟學校)
7. Escola Choi Nong Chi Tai (Choi Nong Chi Tai School/菜農子弟學校)
8. Escola Xin Hua (新華學校)
9. Escola Secundaria Kwong Tai Macau (Kwong Tai Middle School, Macao/廣大中學)
10. Escola Secundária Técnico-Profissional da Associação Geral dos Operários de Macau (澳門工聯職業技術中學)
11. Escola dos Moradores de Macau (澳門坊眾學校)
12. Escola Ling Nam (嶺南中學)
13. Escola Hou Kong (Secundário) (濠江中學)
14. Escola Keang Peng(Secção Secundária) (鏡平學校)
15. Escola dos Moradores de Macau (氹仔坊眾學校)

II. CATHOLIC SCHOOLS

1. Escola de São José de Ká Hó (九澳聖若瑟學校)
2. Escola Nossa Senhora De Fátima (Our Lady Of Fatima Girls' School/化地瑪聖母女子學校)

3. Colégio Mateus Ricci(利瑪竇中學)
4. Escola São João De Brito(庇道學校)
5. Escola Católica Estrela do Mar (海星中學)
6. Colégio Perpétuo Socorro Chan Sui Ki (Chan Sui Ki Perpetual Help College/陳瑞祺永援中學)
7. Instituto Salesiano (慈幼中學)
8. Colégio Yuet Wah (Yuet Wah College/**粵華中學**)
9. Escola Do Santíssimo Rosário (聖玫瑰學校)
10. Escola São Paulo (Saint Paul School Macau/聖保祿學校)
11. Colégio Diocesano de São José (5ª), Cinta Escola (聖若瑟教區中學第五校)
12. Colégio de Santa Rosa de Lima - Secção Chinesa (聖羅撒女子中學中文部)
13. Colégio de Santa Rosa de Lima - Secção Inglesa (Santa Rosa de Lima English Secondary/聖羅撒英文中學)
14. Colégio do Sagrado Coração de Jesus (Sacred Heart Canossian College Chinese Section/嘉諾撒聖心中學)
15. Colégio do Sagrado Coração de Jesus - Secção Inglesa (Sacred Heart Canossian College English Section/嘉諾撒聖心英文中學)
16. Colegio Escola Dom Luis VersigLia (雷鳴道主教紀念學校)

III. Public Schools

1. Escola Secundária Luso-Chinesa de Luís Gonzaga Gomes (高美士中葡中學)
2. Escola Luso-Chinesa Tecnico-Profissional (中葡職業技術學校)
3. Escola Oficial Zheng Guanying(鄭觀應公立學校)

IV. Other Schools

1. Escola Concórdia para Ensino Especial (協同特殊教育學校)
2. Escola Secundária Pui Ching (Pui Ching Middle School/培正中學)

3. Sheng Kung Hui Escola Choi Kou (Macau) (Sheng Kung Hui Choi Kou School (Macau)/聖公會(澳門)蔡高中學)
4. Colegio Anglicano De Macau (Macau Anglican College/聖公會中學)
5. 澳門三育中學Escola Secundária Sam Yuk De Macau / Macao Sam Yuk Middle School (基督教)
6. Escola Cham Son de Macau (澳門浸信中學)
7. Escola das Nações (聯國學校)
8. Escola De Aplicacao Anexa A Universidade De Macau (The Affiliated School of the University of Macau/ 澳門大學附屬應用學校)
9. Escola Internacional de Macau (澳門國際學校)

APPENDIX B. INTERVIEW SCHEDULE (FOCUS-GROUP INTERVIEW WITH TEACHERS)

I. SESSION ONE

A. School regulations

1. Overall

- In general, do you think there is a need for school regulations? Why?
- What is, in your view, the purpose of having school regulations?
- What are the qualities of the ideal student according to your understanding of school regulations? Why do you think so? And, what are the qualities of your ideal student?
- How do school regulations help in shaping your ideal students?
- What do you think about the necessity for a change of school regulations over time?

2. Contents

- Which school regulations do you consider to be good/reasonable? Which school regulations do you consider to be bad/unreasonable? Which school regulations do you consider to be controversial? Why?

- In general, do school regulations rely more on punishment or rewards? What do you think?
- Specifically speaking, how would you like to change them? Any examples? Why?

3. Enforcement

- How do you enforce school regulations (good, bad, controversial)? Do you enforce them with consistence? Elaboration.
- Are there any school regulations that are not enforced? Elaboration.
- Have you come across any difficulties in enforcing school regulations (good, bad, controversial)? Elaboration. How did you resolve them?
- How does the enforcement of school regulations affect the interactions with your students? Elaboration.

B. In-grade retention

1. Overall

- In general, do you think there is a need for in-grade retention? Why?
- What is, in your view, the purpose of having in-grade retention? Why?
- What do you think about the high retention rate in Macao? Do you think that needs to be changed? Why?
- What do you think about the criteria for retention? Are they reasonable or acceptable? Elaboration.
- What changes have you observed about students who are retained?

2. Policy

- DSEJ considers that student assessment could lower the retention rate in Macao. What do you think? Why?
- How do you make sense of multi-dimensional assessment? What do you think about it?

II. Session Two

A. Teacher's ethics

1. Overall

- In general, do you think there is a need for teacher's ethics? Why?
- What is, in your view, the purpose of having teacher's ethics?
- How do teacher's ethics enhance your professionalism?
- How do you see teacher's ethics – is it the minimum requirement or the ideal?
- What are the qualities of your ideal teacher? Why do you think so?

2. Contents

- Which specific item of teacher's ethics do you consider to be good/reasonable? Which specific item of teacher's ethics do you consider to be bad/unreasonable? Which specific item of teacher's ethics do you consider to be controversial? Why
- Specifically speaking, how would you like to change them? Any examples? Why?
- Can students or parents or the public assess the contents of teacher's ethics? What do you think about this issue?

3. Enforcement

- How does your school/management in your school enforce teacher's ethics (good, bad, controversial)? What are consequences of teacher's ethics are violated? Elaboration.
- Are there any cases where students challenge teachers by referring to teacher's ethics? Elaboration.
- Have you come across any unreasonable treatment? Or, have you witnessed some similar cases? Elaboration. How did you/the one concerned handle it?
- How does the enforcement of teacher's ethics affect your interactions with the management, the principal in particular? And how does that affect the interaction between teachers and the management in general? Elaboration.

B. Other views

1. The legal frame of regulating teachers hired by private schools

- How would you comment on its current implementation?
- Have you come across situations where the principles of the legal frame are violated? Elaboration.
- How does it enable your professional development and the professional development of teachers in general? Elaboration.
- Do you feel you are more devoted to the teaching profession after the implementation? Why?

2. Teacher assessment

- According to the legal frame of regulating teachers hired by private schools, teacher assessment will be implemented in the academic year of 2003. What do you think about it?
- In your view, what is the purpose of teacher assessment?
- Do you think this would bring changes to you and teachers in general? Why?

APPENDIX C.
INTERVIEW SCHEDULE
(HIGH SCHOOL STUDENTS)

Date and time of interview: ________________________
Place of interview: ______________________________
Reference number: ______________________________

I. Fill out before the interview (with the interviewer's assistance):

A. Personal information

1. Name: ____________________________
2. Gender: ________
3. Year of birth: _______________________
4. Place of birth: ______________________

B. Previous academic performances

1. Average mark last year: ________
2. Class ranking last year (class size: ____): Top 10 / Bottom 10 / Middle
3. Were you in an elite class: No / Yes
4. Have you ever been retained? No / Yes, (specify when _______)
5. How would you comment on your academic performance?

Excellent / Good / Average / Okay / Poor

C. Anticipation for the next year

1. Expected average mark: _________
2. Expected class ranking (class size: ____): Top 10 / Bottom 10 / Middle

3. Will you be in an elite class: No / Yes
4. Examinations applied:
a. TOFEL / IELTS / SAT / other exams for overseas _______
b. The Public Exam for Mainlanders in Macao
c. The Public Exam for Taiwanese in Macao
d. The Public Exam for Hong Kong people
e. Entrance exams in Macao: UM / MUT / TI / IIUM / others ______
5. Anticipated results for the examinations applied

D. Information about Father
1. Age / Year of birth: ___________________________
2. Place of birth: ___________________________
3. Job title: ___________________________
4. Employment status: employer / employee / self-employed / unemployed
5. Sector: government / public / private / voluntary
6. Level of educational attainment (where):
____

E. Information about Mother
1. Age / Year of birth: ___________________________
2. Place of birth: ___________________________
3. Job title: ___________________________
4. Employment status: employer / employee / self-employed / unemployed
5. Sector: government / public / private / voluntary
6. Level of educational attainment (where):
____

F. Information about Siblings
1. Sibling order: ________
2. Number of siblings (age/gender): _______
sibling 1: Male / Female
year and place of birth: ___________________________
job title: ________________________
employment status: employer / employee / self-employed / unemployed
sector: government / public / private / voluntary
level of educational attainment (where): ___________________________
sibling 2: Male / Female
year and place of birth: ___________________________
job title: ________________________

employment status: employer / employee / self-employed / unemployed
sector: government / public / private / voluntary
level of educational attainment (where): ___________________________
sibling 3: Male / Female
year and place of birth: ___________________________
job title: ________________________
employment status: employer / employee / self-employed / unemployed
sector: government / public / private / voluntary
level of educational attainment (where): ___________________________
sibling 4: Male / Female
year and place of birth: ___________________________
job title: _______________________
employment status: employer / employee / self-employed / unemployed
sector: government / public / private / voluntary
level of educational attainment (where): ___________________________

G. Information about the entire family

1. Total number of family members: ____________
2. Forms of housing: Rented public housing (社屋) / Bought public housing (經屋) / Private housing (私樓) / Others (specify _______________)
3. Types of housing: rented / mortgaged / owned
4. Total monthly income (in MOP)

__ less than 5000
__ 5000 or more but less than 15000
__ 15000 or more but less than 25000
__ 25000 or more but less than 35000
__ 35000 or more but less than 45000
__ 45000 or more but less than 55000
__ more than 55000

II. Areas to be discussed in the interview:

A. Aspirations and future plans

1. Ideally, what educational level would you like to attain? Why? Realistically, what educational level do you expect to attain? Why? Ideally, in which area would you like to specialize? Why? And, realistically, in which area do you expect to specialize? Why?

2. What sort of job would you like to settle in? Why? What is your ideal job? What makes an ideal job?
3. Where would you like to develop your career? Why? Where is an ideal place for you to develop your career? What makes an ideal place?
4. What do you think where you will be staying and what you will be doing in the following year?
5. Given all the options (in section C of Part I) you mentioned at the beginning, what is your priority?
6. What is your plan for the coming five years?

B. Relations with parents

1. Perceived parental expectations

a. What do your parents expect of you?
b. What educational level do your parents want you to attain? Why?
c. In which area do your parents want you to specialize? Why?
d. What sort of job do your parents want you to settle in? Why?
e. What do your parents want you to become?

2. Parental assistance

a. Do you think your parents attach importance to your education? Illustrations.
b. What kind of assistance/support have you received from your parents as to your education? Elaboration.
c. What areas of your education/career did/do you discuss with your parents? Why? Illustrations.
d. Which important educational/career decisions did your parents make for you? Illustrations.
e. What happened when your parents' decisions for you and your own decisions were in conflict? Illustrations.
f. What are your parents' plans for you? Elaboration.
g. How do your parents comment on your educational/career plans? Illustrations.
h. How satisfied are your parents with what you have achieved so far?

3. Communication with parents

a. Would you tell your parents what happen at school? What is it about? Why?

b. Do your parents know your classmates, friends, teachers, etc.? (please name some of them)

c. How often and under what circumstances do you do things together with your parents?

d. How would you describe your relationships with your parents?

C. Educational experience

1. Primary and secondary education

a. What sort of primary school and secondary school did you go to?

b. How would you describe your primary/secondary school life?

c. How do you like schools in Macao?

d. What do you like/enjoy most? Why? What do you consider to be most memorable?

e. What do you like/enjoy least? Why? What do you consider to be most embarrassing or humiliating?

f. What worry you most? Why?

g. What are the most important things that you have learned?

2. Perception of teachers

a. How would you describe your teachers?

b. What did you learn from your teachers? Illustrations. Describe the most memorable incidents concerning your teachers.

c. Name three teachers whom you respected or liked most so far. How did they differ from other teachers? How did you like them? Illustrations.

d. What makes a good teacher?

3. Perception of classmates

a. How would you describe your classmates?

b. What did you learn from your classmates? Illustrations. Describe the most memorable incidents concerning your classmates.

c. Name three classmates whom you consider to be your friends. How do you like them? What do you learn from them? Illustrations.

d. What makes a good friend?

C. Self-evaluation

1. How would you describe yourself as a student? How would you compare yourself with your classmates?
2. Do you consider yourself to be a good / competent / successful student? What makes a good / competent / successful student? Why? Illustrations.
3. What are your major achievements? What are your major setbacks? How satisfied are you with what you have achieved so far?
4. What are your strengths? What are your weaknesses? Which areas do you want to improve on?
5. What do you want to become? Do you see yourself becoming a successful person in the future? Why? What makes a successful person?

D. Perception of education and evaluation of the Macao educational system

1. What do you think the ultimate goals of education?

2. What role of education does it play in Macao?

3. What is the point of getting education? Why do you think so?

4. How do you describe the educational system in Macao? How do you like it?

a. What do you consider to be its strengths? What do you consider to be its weaknesses? Why?

b. What do you like best? What do you like least? Why?

c. Do you consider the system to be fair and just? Why? Illustrations.

d. What needs to be changed? Why?

e. How would you compare it with the system in Hong Kong / the Mainland / Taiwan? Illustrations

5. What are the major issues that deserve societal attention at the moment? Why do you think so?

F. Inequality and Successes in Macao

1. How do you like Macao? What do you like most? What do you like least?
2. What do you think about the gambling industry in Macao? Elaboration.
3. What do you think about the situation of social inequality in Macao? Description / Elaboration.

4. What do you think about social competition in Macao? Do you think it is open and fair? Elaboration.
5. Do you think all people in Macao have an equal chance to become successful? Why? Illustrations.
6. Do you think Macao is a place where people can develop their potential to the full? Why? Illustrations.
7. What are the most important factors leading one to success in Macao?
8. Name someone whom you consider to be successful in Macao. What make you think so? Elaboration.
9. How would you rank the following factors contributing to one's success in Macao (1 the most important and 10 the least important):
   ____ Hardwork
   ____ Training/Qualification
   ____ Innate ability
   ____ Personality
   ____ Ambition
   ____ Social contacts; i.e., knowing the right people
   ____ Wealthy background
   ____ Good upbringing
   ____ Macao born
   ____ Luck

Please leave your contact information for a follow-up telephone interview in August next year:

Phone number: ________________

Email address: ________________

APPENDIX D. INTERVIEW SCHEDULE (EVENING SCHOOL STUDENTS)

The interview will include the following sections but actually will follow naturally the flow of the conversation

I. Background information

1. Name
2. Age
3. Gender
4. Place of birth
5. Which form are you in at this school?
6. What subjects are you doing?
7. Current job (employment status) and income
8. Living arrangements / Form of housing
9. Marital status / information about the spouse/partner (if any) and information about children (if any)
10. Family background
    a. Father
        - Current situation: educational attainments, occupations (employment status), income
        - Educational and work histories
    b. Mother:
        - Current situation: educational attainments, occupations (employment status), income
        - Educational and work histories

c. Siblings (each):
   - Current situation: educational attainments, occupations (employment status), income
   - Educational and work histories

II. Education/Work history before coming to this evening school

1. When did you come to study here?
2. Why did you come to study here?
3. Experience of previous day-school primary/secondary education

- academic life (performances): best-performed subjects; worse-performed subjects
- favourite subjects; hated subjects; why?
- favourite classes; hated classes' why?
- school life (routine activities; memorable events, etc.): How did you like school (rules, set-up, curriculum, pedagogy, etc.)? How did you like your class? (class structure/power dynamics, teacher-student relations, etc.)
- social life: relationships with male/female classmates, with male/female friends, with male/female teachers
- perceptions of classmates/friends (ideal classmates/friends) and of teachers (ideal teachers)
- any problems at school? How did you handle them? Did you turn to any sources of help? Why (or Why not)?
- the happiest moment/scenario? the unhappiest moment/scenario?
- how did you like schools in general?

III. Quitting

1. When did you quit school? Why?
2. What did you do after quitting? What were your plans at the time?
3. How did your family/parents/siblings respond to your decision? What did they do/say?
4. Initially how did you feel about quitting? What happened then? What was your life like after quitting (e.g., routines)? Was it what you had expected or dreamed about? What did you think then? (probing on each of the changes mentioned)
5. When did you decide to return to school? Why? What did you want to achieve by returning school?

IV. Comparison of the school here and the previous school(s)

1. Describe your current school life
2. How do you like the present school?
3. What are the major differences between the school (class) now and those in the past? (teaching missions, curriculum, pedagogies, teachers, classmates, etc.)
4. What do you want to achieve here (e.g., educational level? subjects/areas specialised?)? Why?
5. Do you think it is possible to achieve them? Are there any obstacles? Is there any assistance?

V. Future Plans

1. What are your educational plans? for the immediate future? for the next five years?
2. What are your career plans? for the immediate future? for the next five years?
3. How do you see yourself in the future?

VI. Relationships with parents and siblings over the time

1. Their aspirations/plans for you at different stages
2. Their support (various types) at different stages

VII. Self-evaluation and evaluations of the education system (society)

1. Do you think you have changed? In what ways?
2. If so, how do you like the previous self? Why? (instances?) And, how do you see your new self? What are the differences? (examples?)
3. If you could have a chance to start all over again, what would you have done? Why?
4. What are the turning points over these years? Why do you think so?
5. How do you think about the education system in Macao? How do you like it? Did you enjoy it?
6. How do you like Macao? What do you think about the gambling industry?

APPENDIX E. INTERVIEW SCHEDULE (SCHOOL DROPOUTS)

Date and time of interview: ____________________________
Place of interview: ___________________________________
Reference number: ___________________________________

I. Fill out before the interview (with the interviewer's assistance):

A. Personal information

1. Name: ______________________________
2. Gender: ________
3. Year of birth: ____________________
4. Place of birth: ____________________

B. Previous academic performances

1. School and form enrolled before leaving: ______________________
2. Average mark last year: ________
2. Class ranking last year (class size: ____): Top 10 / Bottom 10 / Middle
3. Were you in an elite class: No / Yes
4. Have you ever been retained? No / Yes, (how many times? ___;
specify when: ___________;
ranking when you were retained: _____________)

C. Information about Father

1. Age / Year of birth: ____________________________
2. Place of birth: ____________________________
3. Job title: ____________________________
4. Employment status:

employee / self-employed / unemployed / employer (with __ employees)

5. Sector: government / public / private / voluntary
6. Level of educational attainment (where): __________________________

D. Information about Mother

1. Age / Year of birth: ____________________________
2. Place of birth: ____________________________
3. Job title: ____________________________
4. Employment status:

employee / self-employed / unemployed / employer (with __ employees)

5. Sector: government / public / private / voluntary
6. Level of educational attainment (where): __________________________

E. Information about the entire family

1. Total number of family members: _____________
2. Forms of housing: Rented public housing (社屋) / Bought public housing (經屋) / Private housing (私樓) / Others (specify _______________)
3. Types of housing: rented / mortgaged / owned
4. Total monthly income (in MOP)

__ less than 5000
__ 5000 or more but less than 15000
__ 15000 or more but less than 25000
__ 25000 or more but less than 35000
__ 35000 or more but less than 45000
__ 45000 or more but less than 55000
__ more than 55000

F. Information about Siblings

1. Sibling order: ________
2. Number of siblings (age/gender): _______

sibling 1: Male / Female

year and place of birth: ____________________________

job title: ________________________

employment status: employer / employee / self-employed / unemployed

sector: government / public / private / voluntary

level of educational attainment (where): ____________________________

ever retained? If yes, how many times? __________________________

sibling 2: Male / Female

year and place of birth: ____________________________

job title: ________________________

employment status: employer / employee / self-employed / unemployed

sector: government / public / private / voluntary

level of educational attainment (where): ___________________________

ever retained? If yes, how many times? __________________________

sibling 3: Male / Female

year and place of birth: ____________________________

job title: _________________________

employment status: employer / employee / self-employed / unemployed

sector: government / public / private / voluntary

level of educational attainment (where): ____________________________

ever retained? If yes, how many times? __________________________

sibling 4: Male / Female

year and place of birth: ____________________________

job title: ________________________

employment status: employer / employee / self-employed / unemployed

sector: government / public / private / voluntary

level of educational attainment (where): ____________________________

ever retained? If yes, how many times? __________________________

II. Areas to be discussed in the interview:

A. Relations with parents

1. Perceived parental expectations

a. What do your parents expect of you?
b. What educational level do your parents want you to attain? Why?
c. What sort of job do your parents want you to settle in? Why?
d. What do your parents want you to become?

2. Parental assistance

a. How do you get along with your parents? Illustrations.
b. Do you think your parents attach importance to your education? Do you think they care about whether you do well at school? Illustrations.
c. (For those who have been retained) How do your parents see your retention? What did they do after you were retained?
d. What kind of assistance/support have you received from your parents (siblings, if applicable) about your education? Elaboration.
e. Did your parents choose schools for you? How did they do that (their considerations)?
f. Did your parents send you to cram school? How much did that cost a month? What were your parents' concerns?
g. Did your parents arrange any extra-curricular activities for you? How much did they spend on those? What did your parents want you to achieve through such activities?
h. What would you discuss with your parents? Would you tell them what happen at school or your problems (academic/behavioral/physical/emotional) at school? Illustrations.
i. Are your parents involved at your school? Would they talk with your teachers about you? Elaboration.

B. Quitting

1. When did you leave school? Why?
2. How did your parents/siblings respond to your quitting? What did they do/say? And, how did you respond to them?
3. Initially how did you feel about leaving school? What happened then? What was your life like after quitting (e.g., routines)? What do you think now?
4. Are you still in touch with teachers/classmates from the previous school(s)? What have your teachers/classmates done about your leaving? How do they see about your leaving (e.g., do they care about it?)? How do you feel about their reactions?
5. What do you think about learning after quitting school? Do you feel it necessary to do some learning on your own? What are the difficulties?

C. School life

1. General

a. What sort of primary school and secondary school did you go to?
b. How would you describe your primary/secondary school life (routines)?
c. What is school life like (routine activities; memorable events, etc.)?
d. How do you like the setup of school (what is taught there, how it is taught there, and how you interact with classmates/friends and teachers)?

2. Academic progress

a. Have you tried to keep up with classes? Illustrations.
b. How far do you understand what is going on in classes? Elaboration.
c. Are you learning in classes? Elaboration.
d. Do you think you can keep up with classes? What do you think about your academic performance/progress? Illustrations.

3. With teachers

a. What are your favourite/hated subjects? Why?
b. What is a typical class like? Elaboration.
c. How do you like your class? Are they interesting? How do you participate in classes? Elaboration.
d. Are teachers teaching in classes?
e. What are your relationships with teachers? Illustrations.
f. Have you ever argued with teachers? Over what issues? What happened in the end? Illustrations.
g. How do you like your teachers? Do you find them helpful in general? Elaboration.
h. Have you met any good teachers? What are they like? What makes an ideal teacher?

4. With classmates/friends

a. What do you do with your classmates/friends in class/during the break/outside of school? Elaboration.
b. How do you like your classmates/friends? What are your relationships with them? Illustrations.
c. How do your classmates/friends feel about teachers or monitors who enforce school regulations?

d. Are you involved in extra-curricular activities? Do you enjoy them? Have you made any friends there? Why?
e. Have you made any friends at all? What are they like? What makes a good friend for you? Would you turn to your classmates/friends for help?

5. With school

a. What do you think about school regulations? Are they necessary? Are they sensible?
b. What do you think about in-grade retention? How do you like it?
c. How often do you break them? Why? Illustrations.
d. What is the point of going to school? Why? Illustrations.
e. Is school a happy place? Why? How do you like school in general?

D. Evaluations

1. Self-evaluation

a. Do you feel good about yourself as a student? Do you feel that everyone puts you down? Do you feel that everyone looks up to you? Illustrations.
b. Do you consider yourself to be a good student? Why? What makes a good student? Illustrations.
c. What are you proud of yourself most? What are you ashamed of yourself most? Elaboration.

2. Evaluation of Macao

d. How do you like Macao? What do you like most? What do you like least?
e. What do you think about the gambling industry in Macao? Have you considered joining the industry? Why? Elaboration.
f. Do you think Macao is a competitive society? Elaboration.
g. Who are your role models/idols in Macao? Why?
h. Do you think education can get you a better future in Macao? Why? Elaboration.
i. Do you think you will get ahead in Macao in the future? Do you think you have a better chance than others? Elaboration.

E. Aspirations and future plans

1. What educational level would you like to attain? Why?
2. How do you like studies? Why? Are you satisfied with your studies/education? Why?
3. What sort of job would you like to settle in? Why? What is your ideal job?
4. What is your immediate plan?
5. What is your plan for the coming five years?
6. How would you like to live your life in the future? What do you want to achieve in the future? Why?

REFERENCES

Articles and Books (in English)

Bray, M. (2002) Higher Education in Macau: Growth and Strategic Development, Hong Kong: Comparative Education Research Centre, the University of Hong Kong.

Bray, M. (1992) 'Colonialism, Scale, and Politics: Divergence and Convergence of Educational Development in Hong Kong and Macau' Comparative Education Review 36(3): 322-342.

Bray, M. and Koo, R. (eds) (2004) Education and Society in Hong Kong and Macao: Comparative Perspectives on Continuity and Change, Second Edition, Hong Kong: Comparative Education Research Centre, University of Hong Kong, and Kluwer Academic Publishers.

Choi, B. and Koo, R. (eds) (2001) Education and Social Development in Macau, Hong Kong: Hong Kong Institute of Education.

Clayton, C. (2009) Sovereignty at the Edge: Macau and the Question of Chineseness, Cambridge (Mass.) and London: the Harvard University Asia Center.

Giddens, A. (2001) Sociology, Fourth Edition, Cambridge: Polity.

Gunn, G.C. (1996) Encountering Macau: A Portuguese City-State on the Periphery of China, 1557-1999, Boulder, CO: Westview Press, Inc.

Ingersoll, R.M. and Perda, D. (2008) 'The Status of Teaching as a Profession' in J.H. Ballantine and J.Z. Spade (eds) Schools and Society, Third Edition, LA: Pine Forge Press.

Jimerson, S.R., Anderson, G.E., and Whipple, A.A.D. (2002) 'Winning the Battle and Losing the War: Examining the Relation between Grade Retention and Dropping Out of High School' Psychology in the Schools 39(4): 441-457

Lam, N. and Scott, I. (eds) (2011) Gaming, governance and public policy in Macao, Hong Kong: Hong Kong University Press.

Porter, J. (1996) Macau, the imaginary city, Boulder, CO.: Westview Press.

Ream, R.K. and Rumberger, R.W. (2008) Student Engagement, Peer Social Capital, and School Dropout Among Mexican American and Non-Latino White Students' Sociology of Education 81(2): 109-139.

Roderick, M. (1994) 'Grade Retention and School Dropout: Investigating the Association' American Educational Research Journal 31(4): 729-759.

Roderick, M. and Nagaoka, J. (2005) 'Retention Under Chicago's High-Stakes Testing Program: Helpful, Harmful, or Harmless?' Educational Evaluation and Policy Analysis 27(4): 309-340.

Wang, H. Y., Kong, M., Shan, W. J., and Vong, S. K. (2010) 'The effects of doing part-time jobs on college student academic performance and social life in a Chinese society' Journal of Education and Work 23: 79-94.

Wong, Y.L. (2013) 'Why are In-grade Retention Rates so High in Macao?' Current Issues in Education, 16(3) http://cie.asu.edu/ojs/index.php/cieatasu/article/view/1240/537

ARTICLES AND BOOKS (IN CHINESE)

Chan, C. F. (ed) (2010): "The return of Macao decade Memorabilia category of non-tertiary education." Macau: Macao and China Education Association. 陳志峰(編)(2010) : 《澳門回歸十年非高等教育範疇大事記》。澳門： 澳門中華教育會

Chan, C. F. and Ieong, P. Y. (eds) (2012): "Macao and Africa Higher Education Laws and Regulations common areas." Beijing: China Social Sciences Press. 陳志峰、楊珮欣(編) (2012) 《澳門非高等教育範疇常用法律法規匯編》。 北京：中國社會科學出版社

Chan, C. Y. (2011): "Citizen Participation and civic consciousness" to close at Fanny Cheung, Wong Siu-lun, Yin Baoshan, Zhenghong Tai (ed) "the Macao SAR new look". Hong Kong: Chinese University of Hong Kong Institute of Asia. 陳振宇(2011) 〝公民参與和公民意識〞 收於張妙清、黃紹倫、尹寶珊、鄭宏泰(編) 《澳門特區新貌》香港：香港中文大學香港亞太研究所。

Cheng, W.T., and Wong, S.L. (2014): "Reflections on the implementation of good governance and recommendations to close" at Fanny Cheung, Wong

Siu-lun, Yin Baoshan, Zhenghong Tai (ed). “Building Macau future.” Hong Kong: Chinese University of Hong Kong Institute of Asia. 鄭宏泰、黃紹倫(2014) 〝落實良好管治的思考與建議〞收於張妙清、黃紹倫、尹寶珊、鄭宏泰(編)《構建澳門未來》。香港：香港中文大學香港亞太研究所。

Cheung, F. Wong S. L., Yin B., Zhenghong T. (eds) (2014): “Building Macau future.” Hong Kong: Chinese University of Hong Kong Institute of Asia. 張妙清、黃紹倫、尹寶珊、鄭宏泰(編)(2014) 《構建澳門未來》。香港：香港中文大學香港亞太研究所。

Cheung, F. Wong S. L., Yin B., Zhenghong T. (eds) (2011): “The Macao SAR new look.” Hong Kong: Chinese University of Hong Kong Institute of Asia. .張妙清、黃紹倫、尹寶珊、鄭宏泰(編)(2011)《澳門特區新貌》。香港：香港中文大學香港亞太研究所。

DSEJ (1994): “Macao school characteristics.” Macau: Macau Education and Youth Division published. 澳門教育暨青年司(1994)《澳門學校特徵》。澳門：澳門教育暨青年司出版

Hung, P.W., and Ip, K.H. (2014): KONG Bao-hua, Yeguo Hao (2014) “associations and civil society development” close at Fanny Cheung, Wong Siu-lun, Yin Baoshan, Zhenghong Tai (ed). “Building Macau future.” Hong Kong: Chinese University of Hong Kong Institute of Asia.孔寶華、葉國豪(2014) 〝社團與公民社會的發展〞收於張妙清、黃紹倫、尹寶珊、鄭宏泰(編)《構建澳門未來》。香港：香港中文大學香港亞太研究所。

Ng, C. L. et al. (eds) (2008): “A History of Macao.” Macau: Macau Foundation. 吳志良、金國平、湯開建(編)(2008) 《澳門史新編》。澳門：澳門基金會

Wang, K. Y. et al. (eds) (2009): Wang J., Wong S. L., Yin B., Zhenghong T. (eds) (2014), “Macao society new look.” Hong Kong: Chinese University of Hong Kong Institute of Asia. 王家英、黃紹倫、尹寶珊、鄭宏泰(編)(2014) 《澳門社會新貌》。香港：香港中文大學香港亞太研究所

Wong, H. K. (ed) (1991): “Macao education reform.” Macau: Macau University of East Asia Research Center. 黃漢強(編)(1991)《澳門教育改革》。澳門：東亞大學澳門研究中心

Wong, S. L., Yeung, Yin B., Zhenghong T. (eds) (2007), “Macao society new look.” Hong Kong: Chinese University of Hong Kong Institute of Asia.

黃紹倫、楊汝萬、尹寶珊、鄭宏泰(編)(2007)《澳門社會新貌》。香港：香港中文大學香港亞太研究所

Yu, C. and Lui, K.M. (2007): “public political culture” to close at Wong S. L., Yeung, Yin B., Zhenghong T. (ed) “Macao society new look.” Hong Kong: Chinese University of Hong Kong Institute of Asia. 余振、呂國民(2007) 〝大眾政治文化〞收於黃紹倫、楊汝萬、尹寶珊、鄭宏泰(編)《澳門社會新貌》。香港：香港中文大學香港亞太研究所

NON-OFFICIAL DOCUMENTS

Macao Daily (www.macaodaily.com), clippings:

3 December 2007: “The reason I joined the procession of teachers”《我参加教師遊行的原因》

25 February 2008: “Teacher absence of Educational Planning”《教師缺席教育規劃》

2 May 2011: “Two thousand three parade table aspirations.” 《二千三人遊行表訴求》

3 May 2011: “Implementing the private box steady teachers”《落實私框穩教師隊伍》

16 May 2011a: “Scholars called on the private box legislation as soon as possible”《學者籲私框盡快立法》

16 May 2011b: “Plus gas pressure difficult Teo”《八方壓力難啉氣》

19 March 2012: “On the private box”《淺談私框》

29 May 2013: “Teacher's Convention Watch Group was established”《教師公約關注小組成立》

OECD (2010) *PISA 2009 Results*.

OECD (2007) *PISA 2006 Results*.

OECD (2004) *PISA 2003 Results*.

OFFICIAL DOCUMENTS

Macao SAR Statistics and Census Service (http://www.dsec.gov.mo)

Education and Youth Affairs Bureau (http://www.dsej.gov.mo)

INDEX

A

B

C

D

E

F

G

H

I

J

K

L

M

T

U

V

W

Y